HOME BAKING

HOME BAKING

CONSULTING EDITOR:
MARTHA DAY

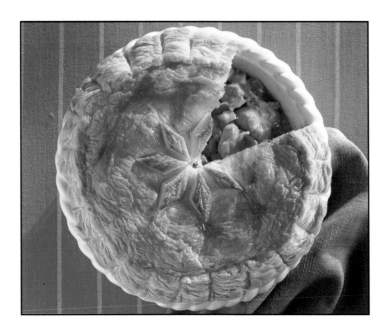

LORENZ BOOKS

First published in 1999 by Lorenz Books

© Anness Publishing Limited 1999

LORENZ BOOKS are available for bulk purchase for sales promotion and for premium use.
For details, write or call the sales director, Lorenz Books, 27 West 20th Street,
New York, NY 10011; (800) 354-9657

Lorenz Books is an imprint of Anness Publishing Inc.

ISBN 0 7548 0290 6

Publisher Joanna Lorenz
Project Editor Emma Hardy
Designer Lilian Lindblom
Illustrator Anna Koska
Photographers Karl Adamson, Michael Michaels, James Duncan, Steve Baxter, Amanda
Heywood, Michelle Garrett, Don Last & Patrick McLeavey
Recipes Christine France, Roz Denny, Catherine Atkinson, Liz Trigg, Rosamund Grant,
Sarah Gates, Carole Clements, Elizabeth Wolf-Cohen, Nicola Diggins, Patricia Lousada,
Frances Cleary, Sallie Morris, Shirley Gill & Norma MacMillan

Printed and bound in Singapore

1 3 5 7 9 10 8 6 4 2

Contents

Introduction

At a time where so much of what we buy is pre-packed, when cookies come in rolls with tag-pulls for easy opening, freezers are filled with fudge cakes, and ready-to-fill pastry shells are on sale in every grocery store, maybe it is time to campaign for a return to home baking. Remember the smell of newly baked bread, the welcome sight of a batch of fresh scones, the taste of homemade bread packed with candied fruits? These are treats few commercial products can match, and if the demands of modern living mean we seldom have time to bake our own cookies, perhaps we need to look again at how we use the time we have. Baking is one of the most satisfying branches of cooking. Kneading dough can

be very therapeutic after a day dealing with difficult clients or demanding children, and the repetitive tasks of rolling out dough, and cutting out cookies can be positively soothing as an antidote to rush hour travel. Much has been made of the dangers of a diet high in fats and sugars. When you do your own baking, you have far more control over what your family eats. Reducing the amount of refined sugar in cakes and cookies is easy to achieve, especially if you use dried fruits. Low-fat lunchbox treats, like Apricot Yogurt Cookies on page 58, are a much better bet than chocolate bars.

Home baking doesn't have to be horribly time-consuming. Bread is a cinch thanks to dried yeast, which is added directly to the dry ingredients. You can make the dough in a food processor or blender, if you choose, and as it only needs a single proving, baking a loaf of bread or a dozen rolls is simplicity itself.

Many of the cakes and quick breads in this book take very little time to produce, and even pastry, which some people regard as fiddly, is child's play if you remember these few cardinal rules: when you rub fat into flour, work fast, and lift the mixture to incorporate air; add only enough liquid to enable the ingredients to bind together; handle the dough as little as possible, and roll it out quickly and lightly. Lining pie pans, spooning in filling, and adding pastry lids can take time, especially if you crimp the edges and decorate the top of the pie, but there's no need to do any of that if you are in a hurry. Just roll out a large circle to fit the pie pan with plenty of overlap, add your filling, and place the extra pastry over. It won't cover the filling completely but that doesn't matter—the rustic effect is part of the charm. The Open Apple Pie on page 95 is made by this method, and very good it is too.

For special occasions try some of the more elaborate cakes like the Chocolate Fudge Torte on page 118 or even the Raspberry & Hazelnut Meringue Cake on page 114. Either of these would make a stunning, delicious centerpiece for a celebration tea or a fitting finale to a very special dinner party.

Baking Ingredients

SUGAR
Granulated is an all-purpose sugar. Use superfine for creaming because it dissolves faster, and gives a lighter result. Brown sugar is favored for its flavor in fruit cakes.

BAKING POWDER
Made from baking soda, selected acids and starch, this is an effective raising agent, and is added to flour.

BAKING SODA
This raising agent produces a rapid rise in the presence of an acid. Cakes containing baking soda should be baked as soon as possible after mixing.

DRIED FRUIT
An invaluable pantry ingredient, dried fruit is sold pre-cleaned and seeded for use in cakes and desserts.

FLOUR
Most of the recipes in this book use self-rising, bread or all-purpose flour. Where sifted whole-wheat flour is stipulated, return the bran from the sifter to the bowl.

NUTS
Buy nuts only when you need them if possible, as they can become rancid if kept too long. Opened packages can be stored in the fridge or freezer.

EGGS

Unless recipes specify otherwise, use large eggs. Keep them point-downward in their box in the fridge, allowing them to come to room temperature before use. Always buy eggs from a reputable supplier.

BUTTER

For rich cakes and pastries, butter is the fat of choice. Two types are available—sweet cream butter and lactic butter, the latter tasting slightly more acidic.

MARGARINE

For most cake mixtures, margarine gives good results. Bring block margarine to room temperature before creaming, but use soft margarine straight from the fridge.

OILS

Choose light oils with no discernible flavor for baking. Sunflower oil is ideal, but peanut oil or vegetable oil are also fine for most baking purposes.

YEAST

Breads and some cakes use yeast as the raising agent. The recent development of fast-rising yeast has revolutionized home baking because it is so quick and simple to use, although some cooks still prefer to bake with fresh yeast. A third kind of yeast, active dry yeast, has now largely been replaced by fast-rising yeast.

Types of Pastry

PHYLLO

This traditional Greek pastry comes ready rolled in paper-thin sheets, which are layered, then cooked until crisp. Phyllo is made with very little fat, so each layer must be brushed with oil or melted butter. It dries out quickly when exposed to air, so any pastry not in use should be kept covered with a clean damp dish towel. Bake a phyllo pie as soon as it is assembled.

PUFF PASTRY

This delectable pastry is made in such a way that it separates into crisp, melt-in-the-mouth layers when cooked, thanks to air trapped in the pastry. A block of butter is wrapped in a basic dough; the pastry is then turned, rolled, folded and chilled several times. Although some cooks continue to prepare their own puff pastry, many prefer to buy it ready-made and frozen. Thaw slowly (see package instructions).

FLAKY PASTRY

Similar to puff pastry, but easier to prepare, this involves making a dough with half the stipulated amount of butter, then softening the rest to the same consistency as the dough and dotting some of it all over the surface of the rolled out rectangle of pastry. The pastry is folded, turned and rolled and the process is repeated. When the pastry is baked in a hot oven it separates into crisp leaves that are beautifully light.

ROUGH PUFF

The easiest flaky pastry of all: diced shortening is mixed with flour but not rubbed in, so that when the liquid is added a dough is formed in which the shortening can be seen. The pastry is rolled and folded several times before resting and baking. The shortening should be very cold and it is helpful if the flour is chilled before use.

SHORTCRUST

One of the easiest of pastries, shortcrust consists of flour and fat, with just enough liquid to bind the ingredients together. The standard recipe is to sift 1½ cups all-purpose flour and a pinch of salt into a bowl, then rub in 6 tablespoons diced butter or solid block margarine until it forms fine crumbs. Drizzle 2–3 tablespoons ice water over the surface, then quickly fork it through until the pastry clumps together and can be shaped into a ball. If time permits, wrap shortcrust pastry in plastic and chill it for 30 minutes before rolling it out.

RICH SHORTCRUST

Richer than plain shortcrust, this makes a crisper crust. It is often used for fruit pies. Use the standard shortcrust recipe but make it with 8 tablespoons butter and substitute an egg yolk for part of the liquid. For a sweet pastry, add 2–3 tablespoons sugar after rubbing in the butter.

COOK'S TIPS

To make a quick all-in-one pastry using margarine, cream ½ cup margarine with ¼ cup all-purpose flour and 1 tablespoon cold water. Add another 1¼ cups flour and a pinch of salt and knead to form a smooth dough. Wrap and chill before use.

Make a batch of rubbed-in mixture for shortcrust pastry (without adding any liquid), put it in a plastic container and store it in the freezer. Next time you want to make a pie, just thaw, add water and roll out.

If you prefer to use whole-wheat flour but find it makes your pastry rather chewy, use half whole-wheat and half all-purpose flour.

Spicy pastry is perfect for apple pie. Make a rich shortcrust, but add 1 teaspoon each of ground allspice and cinnamon for every 1 cup flour.

Baking Techniques

KNEADING

Working yeast dough by folding it toward you, then pushing it down and away with the heel of one or both hands. The dough is turned, and the action repeated, often for several minutes, until it feels elastic and no longer sticky.

FOLDING

Lightly mixing an aerated ingredient such as whisked egg whites into other ingredients so that the air does not escape. A metal spoon or a rubber spatula is used with a very light up-and-over action, turning the bowl as you work.

CREAMING

Beating together softened fats with sugar, using a wooden spoon or electric whisk, to make a mixture that resembles whipped cream.

RUBBING-IN

The diced fat (usually butter) is added to the flour, then rubbed between the fingertips until the mixture resembles bread crumbs.

RISING

Putting the dough in a covered bowl (or the baking pan), covering, and setting aside in a warm place until doubled in bulk.

LINING A ROUND PAN

Draw two circles on wax or nonstick parchment paper to fit the bottom of the pan, and cut out. Then cut a long strip slightly longer than the circumference of the pan and about 2 inches taller. Crease the paper strip about 1 inch from a long side, then snip the paper diagonally at intervals from edge to fold. Grease the pan lightly with oil, and fit one of the paper circles in the bottom. Then fit the long strip around the inside with the snipped fringe overlapping neatly at the bottom. Brush lightly with oil, then fit the second paper circle in place at the bottom of the pan.

LINING A SQUARE PAN

Cut a piece of wax or nonstick parchment paper big enough to cover the bottom of the pan and come up the sides, adding an extra 1 inch all around. Center the pan on the paper, then make four cuts in from the side of the paper to the corners of the pan. Overlap the corners of the paper to construct a box the same shape as the pan. Grease the pan, and then fit the paper lining in place.

13

TIME-SAVING TIP

Freeze appropriate amounts of rubbed-in mixture. Defrost when needed, and use for cakes, pastries or crumble toppings. Add sugar and spice as required.

Breads
&
Rolls

Nothing is more evocative than the tantalizing aroma of fresh home baking. From aromatic Olive & Oregano Bread to irresistible Clover Leaf Rolls, this chapter includes an enticing selection of the most delicious breads and rolls.

White Bread

INGREDIENTS

2 tablespoons butter
2 cups milk
7 cups white bread flour
2 teaspoons salt
1 teaspoon sugar
1 tablespoon fast-rising dried yeast
beaten egg, for glazing

MAKES 2 LOAVES

16

1 Melt the butter in the milk in a saucepan. Pour into a pitcher and cool slightly. Sift the flour into a large mixing bowl and stir in the salt, sugar and yeast. Make a well in the center and add the milk mixture. Mix to a soft dough.

2 Lightly grease two 1-pound loaf pans. Knead the dough on a lightly floured surface for about 10 minutes, or until it is smooth and elastic. Divide the dough  in half, shape each half into a loaf and place in the prepared loaf pans.

3 Slip the pans into a large, lightly oiled plastic bag and leave them to rise in a warm place for about 1 hour or until the loaves have doubled in bulk.

4 Preheat the oven to 400°F. Glaze the loaves with beaten egg and bake for 40–45 minutes or until well risen and golden brown. Turn out and cool on a wire rack.

Whole Wheat Bread

INGREDIENTS

1¾ cups water
2 tablespoons clear honey
5¼ cups whole-wheat flour
2 teaspoons salt
4 teaspoons fast-rising dried yeast
¾ cup wheat germ
3 tablespoons corn oil
milk, for glazing

MAKES I LOAF

1 Heat the water in a small pan to simmering point. Stir in the honey until dissolved. Pour into a pitcher and cool slightly.

2 Combine the flour, salt, yeast and wheat germ in a mixing bowl. Make a well in the center and pour in the oil, with enough liquid to make a soft dough.

3 Lightly grease a I-pound loaf pan. Knead the dough on a lightly floured surface for 10 minutes. Shape into a loaf and place in the prepared pan. Slip the pan into a lightly oiled plastic bag and leave the loaf to rise in a warm place for about I hour or until doubled in bulk. Preheat the oven to 400°F

4 Glaze the loaf with the milk. Bake for between 35 and 40 minutes until the crust is golden brown. The loaf should sound hollow when tapped underneath. Allow to cool on a wire rack.

17

Multi-grain Bread

INGREDIENTS

generous ¾ cup rolled oats
2½ cups milk
4 tablespoons sunflower oil
⅓ cup light brown sugar
2 tablespoons clear honey
4 cups bread flour
2 cups soy flour
3 cups whole-wheat flour
½ cup wheat germ
2 teaspoons salt
2 x ¼-ounce envelopes fast-rising dried yeast
2 eggs, lightly beaten

MAKES 2 LOAVES

I Place the oats in a large bowl. In a saucepan, bring the milk to just below boiling point. Pour the hot milk over the oats, then stir in the oil, sugar and honey.

2 Allow the oat mixture to cool. Combine all of the flours, and the wheat germ, salt and yeast in a large mixing bowl. Add the oat mixture and eggs, and mix to a rough dough. Knead on a lightly floured surface for about 10 minutes, until smooth and elastic.

3 Grease two 9 x 5-inch loaf pans. Divide the dough into four equal pieces, and roll each to a cylinder slightly longer than the pan and 1½ inches thick. Twist the cylinders together in pairs, and place in the pans. Cover loosely, and let rise in a warm place until doubled in size.

4 Preheat the oven to 425°F. Bake the loaves for about 30–35 minutes, or until the bottom of each of the loaves sounds hollow when it is lightly tapped. (Tap the bottom of both of the loaves by clenching your hand together to make a fist, and hold the top of the loaf with your other hand.) Cool on a rack.

18

Rye Bread

INGREDIENTS

2 cups water
2 tablespoons molasses
3 cups whole-wheat flour
2 cups rye flour
1 cup white bread flour
1½ teaspoons salt
¼-ounce sachet fast-rising dried yeast
2 tablespoons caraway seeds
2 tablespoons sunflower oil

MAKES 2 LOAVES

1 Heat the water in a small pan to simmering point. Stir in the molasses until dissolved. Pour into a pitcher and cool slightly.

2 Sift the three kinds of flour into a large mixing bowl. Stir in the salt and yeast. Set 1 teaspoon of the caraway seeds aside and add the rest to the bowl.

3 Make a well in the center. Then add the oil, with enough of the warm liquid to make a soft dough. Add a little more of the liquid if necessary.

4 Knead the dough on a lightly floured surface for 10 minutes, until smooth and elastic. Divide in half and shape each piece into a 9-inch long oval loaf.

5 Grease a large cookie sheet. Put the loaves on the sheet, leaving room for rising. Flatten them slightly. Slide the cookie sheet into a lightly oiled large plastic bag and leave in a warm place for up to 2 hours, until the dough has doubled in bulk. Preheat the oven to 400°F.

6 Brush the loaves with water and sprinkle with the reserved caraway seeds. Bake for 30 minutes or until well risen. The loaves should sound hollow when tapped underneath. Cool on a wire rack.

Cheese Bread

INGREDIENTS

2 tablespoons butter
1 cup milk
3 cups white bread flour
2 teaspoons salt
¼-ounce sachet fast-rising dried yeast
1 cup grated mature
Cheddar cheese

MAKES 1 LOAF

1 Melt the butter in the milk in a saucepan. Pour into a pitcher and cool slightly. Sift the flour into a large mixing bowl and stir in the salt and yeast. Make a well in the center and add the milk mixture. Mix to a soft dough.

2 Knead the dough on a lightly floured surface for 10 minutes, then pat it flat and sprinkle with the grated Cheddar cheese. Gather up the dough and knead again to distribute the cheese evenly.

3 Lightly grease a loaf pan. Twist the dough, form into a loaf shape and place in the pan, tucking the ends under. Cover loosely and leave in a warm place for about 1 hour, until doubled in bulk.

4 Preheat the oven to 400°F. Bake the loaf for 15 minutes, then lower the heat to 375°F and bake for 20–30 minutes more, or until the bottom sounds hollow when tapped. Cool on a wire rack.

VARIATION
Try this recipe with grated Monterey Jack cheese, Gruyère or Jarlsberg for a delicious alternative.

22

Dill Bread

INGREDIENTS

4 tablespoons olive oil
½ onion, chopped
7–8 cups white bread flour
2 teaspoons salt
1 tablespoon sugar
2 x ¼-ounce sachets fast-rising
dried yeast
1 large bunch dill, finely chopped
2 eggs, lightly beaten
½ cup cottage cheese
2 cups hand-hot water
milk, for glazing

MAKES 2 LOAVES

1 Heat 1 tablespoon of the olive oil in a small frying pan and fry the onion until soft. Set aside to cool. Lightly grease a large cookie sheet.

2 Combine the flour, salt, sugar and yeast in a large mixing bowl. Make a well in the center and add the onion (with the cooking oil), dill, eggs, cottage cheese and remaining oil. Stir in enough of the hand-hot water to make a soft dough.

3 Knead the dough on a lightly floured surface, until smooth and elastic. Divide in half and shape each piece into a circle.

4 Place the circles of dough on the cookie sheet, cover loosely and leave to rise in a warm place for about 1 hour or until doubled in bulk. Preheat the oven to 375°F.

5 Score the tops of the loaves, glaze with milk and bake for about 45 minutes, until browned. Allow the loaves to cool slightly on a wire rack before serving.

23

Olive & Oregano Bread

INGREDIENTS

1 tablespoon olive oil
1 onion, finely chopped
4 cups white bread flour, plus extra
for dusting
1 teaspoon salt
¼ teaspoon ground black pepper
1 teaspoon fast-rising dried yeast
⅓ cup pitted black olives,
coarsely chopped
1 tablespoon black olive paste
1 tablespoon chopped fresh oregano
1 tablespoon chopped fresh parsley
1¼ cups hand-hot water

MAKES 1 LOAF

24

1 Heat the olive oil in a frying pan. Add the onion and fry over medium heat for 4–5 minutes, until golden. Grease a large cookie sheet.

2 Sift the flour and salt into a large mixing bowl. Stir in the pepper and yeast. Make a well in the center and add the fried onion (with the cooking oil), olives, olive paste and herbs. Stir in enough of the hand-hot water to make a soft dough, adding a little more water if necessary.

3 Transfer the dough to a lightly floured surface and knead for 10 minutes, until smooth and elastic. Shape to an 8-inch circle and place on the prepared cookie sheet.

4 Using a sharp knife, make criss-cross cuts over the top of the dough. Slip the cookie sheet into a lightly oiled plastic bag and leave the loaf to rise in a warm place for about 1 hour, until doubled in bulk. Preheat the oven to 425°F.

5 Dust the loaf with a little flour. Bake for about 10 minutes, then lower the oven temperature to 400°F and bake for 20 minutes more. The loaf is ready when it sounds hollow when tapped underneath. Let the loaf cool for a while on a wire rack. Serve warm.

COOK'S TIP
This bread is delicious served with minestrone or a simple tomato and mozzarella salad.

Sage Soda Bread

INGREDIENTS

2 cups whole-wheat flour
1 cup white bread flour
½ teaspoon salt
1 teaspoon baking soda
2 tablespoons shredded fresh
sage leaves
1¼–1¾ cups buttermilk

MAKES 1 LOAF

1 Preheat the oven to 425°F. Lightly oil a cookie sheet and set aside. Sift both kinds of flour into a bowl and pour in any bran remaining in the sifter. Then stir in the salt, baking soda and sage.

2 Add enough of the buttermilk to make a soft dough, mixing just enough to combine the ingredients. Shape the dough into a circle and place on the cookie sheet.

3 Cut a deep cross in the top of the loaf. Bake for 40 minutes or until the loaf is well risen and sounds hollow when tapped underneath. Cool on a wire rack. Serve warm, with butter.

Zucchini Crown Bread

INGREDIENTS

1 pound zucchini
salt
5 cups white bread flour
2 x ¼-ounce sachets fast-rising
dried yeast
⅔ cup grated Parmesan cheese
ground black pepper
2 tablespoons olive oil
1¼ cups hand-hot water
milk, for glazing
sesame seeds, for the topping

MAKES I LOAF

1 Trim the ends of the zucchini, then grate them into a colander. Sprinkle each layer lightly with salt. Leave to drain for 30 minutes, then rinse, drain and pat dry.

2 Grease and line a 9-inch round cake pan. Mix the flour, yeast and Parmesan in a large mixing bowl. Season with black pepper.

3 Stir in the oil and zucchini and add enough of the hand-hot water to make a fairly firm dough. Knead on a lightly floured surface for 10 minutes. Return to the clean bowl, cover and leave in a warm place to rise for 1 hour or until doubled in bulk.

4 Shape the dough into eight rolls. Fit them into the cake pan, brush the tops with the milk and sprinkle with sesame seeds. Allow the dough rolls to rise again.

5 Preheat the oven to 400°F. Bake the bread for 25 minutes or until golden brown. Let the bread cool on a wire rack.

Parma Ham & Parmesan Bread

INGREDIENTS

2 cups self-rising whole-
wheat flour
2 cups self-rising white flour
1 teaspoon baking powder
1 teaspoon salt
1 teaspoon ground black pepper
3 ounces Parma ham, chopped
⅓ cup grated Parmesan cheese
2 tablespoons chopped fresh parsley
3 tablespoons whole-grain mustard
1½ cups buttermilk, plus
extra for glazing

MAKES I LOAF

28

1 Preheat the oven to 400°F. Lightly flour a cookie sheet and set aside. Place the whole wheat-flour in a bowl and sift in the white flour, baking powder and salt. Stir in the pepper and the Parma ham. Set aside about I tablespoon of the grated Parmesan and stir the rest into the mixture, with the parsley. Make a well in the center of the flour mixture.

2 Mix the mustard and buttermilk in a pitcher, pour on to the flour mixture and quickly mix to a soft dough. Knead briefly on a lightly floured surface, then shape the dough into an oval loaf.

3 Brush the loaf with buttermilk, sprinkle with the reserved Parmesan and place on the cookie sheet. Bake for 25–30 minutes, or until golden brown. Cool on a wire rack.

COOK'S TIP

If you can't locate buttermilk, use lightly soured milk instead. Stir 1 teaspoon lemon juice into 1½ cups milk. Set aside for 15 minutes before use.

Corn Bread

INGREDIENTS

1 cup all-purpose flour
6 tablespoons sugar
1 teaspoon salt
1 tablespoon baking powder
1½ cups cornmeal
1½ cups milk
2 eggs
6 tablespoons butter, melted
½ cup solid margarine, melted

MAKES 1 LOAF

1 Preheat the oven to 400°F. Grease a 1-pound loaf pan and line the bottom with a sheet of baking parchment.

2 Sift the flour, sugar, salt and baking powder into a large mixing bowl. Stir in the cornmeal. Make a well in the center of the flour with a wooden spoon.

3 Whisk the milk and eggs with the melted butter and margarine until well blended. Pour the mixture into the well in the flour mixture. Stir until just blended; do not overmix or the baked bread will not be light.

4 Pour the mixture into the prepared pan and bake for about 45 minutes, or until a skewer inserted in the center of the loaf comes out clean. Turn on to a wire rack. Serve hot or at room temperature. The bread makes an excellent accompaniment to a Mexican meal.

Sesame Seed Bread

INGREDIENTS

1 ½ cups all-purpose white flour
1 ½ cups whole-wheat flour
1 teaspoon salt
2 teaspoons fast-rising dried yeast
1 ¼ cups hand-hot water
½ cup toasted sesame seeds
milk, for glazing
2 tablespoons sesame seeds, for sprinkling

MAKES 1 LOAF

4 Glaze the loaf with the milk and sprinkle with the sesame seeds. Bake for 15 minutes, then lower the oven temperature to 375°F and bake for about 30 minutes more, until the loaf is golden and sounds hollow when tapped underneath. Cool on a wire rack.

1 Sift the flours into a large mixing bowl, then stir in the salt and yeast. Make a well in the center and stir in enough of the hand-hot water to make a rough dough.

2 Knead the dough on a lightly floured surface for 10 minutes, or until smooth and elastic. Knead in the sesame seeds until evenly distributed.

3 Grease a 9-inch cake pan. Divide the dough into 16 balls and fit them side by side in the tin. Cover with a lightly oiled plastic bag and leave in a warm place for about 1 hour, or until the loaf has risen to above the rim of the pan. Preheat the oven to 425°F.

Poppy Seed Knots

INGREDIENTS

1 ½ cups milk
¼ cup sweet butter
6 cups bread flour
2 teaspoons salt
¼-ounce envelope fast-rising dried yeast
1 egg yolk
1 egg, to glaze
2 teaspoons water
poppy seeds (see method)

MAKES 18

1 Heat the milk and butter in a saucepan, stirring occasionally, until the butter has melted. Pour into a pitcher, and cool slightly.

2 Sift the flour and salt into a bowl. Stir in the yeast. Make a well in the center, and add the milk mixture and the egg yolk. Mix to a soft dough. Knead on a lightly floured surface for about 10 minutes, until smooth and elastic but not sticky.

3 Grease a large cookie sheet. Divide the dough into 18 pieces, about the size of golf balls. Roll each piece into a rope, and twist to form a knot. Place the knots 1 inch apart on the cookie sheet. Cover loosely, and let rise in a warm place until the knots have doubled in size.

4 Preheat the oven to 450°F. Beat the egg with the water in a cup. Brush the glaze over the knots, and sprinkle with the poppy seeds. Bake for 12–15 minutes or

until the tops of the knots are lightly browned. Transfer the knots to a rack, and let cool slightly before serving warm.

Clover Leaf Rolls

INGREDIENTS

1¼ cups milk
¼ cup sweet butter
4–5 cups bread flour
2 teaspoons salt
2 tablespoons sugar
¼-ounce sachet fast-rising dried yeast
1 egg, beaten
melted butter, for glazing

MAKES 24

32

1 Place the milk and butter in a saucepan, and heat, stirring occasionally, until the butter has melted. Pour into a pitcher, and cool to hand-hot.

2 Sift 4 cups of the bread flour with the salt into a large bowl. Stir in the sugar and yeast. Make a well in the center, and add the milk and butter mixture. Then add the beaten egg. Mix to a rough dough, adding more flour if necessary. Knead on a lightly floured surface for about 10 minutes, until the dough is smooth, elastic and no longer sticky.

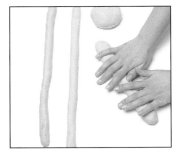

3 Grease two 12-cup muffin pans with a small amount of oil. Divide the dough into four equal pieces, and, with your hands, roll each piece to a rope about 14 inches long. Cut each rope into 18 pieces, and form each piece into a small ball.

4 Place three of the balls, side by side, in each muffin cup. Cover loosely, and let rise in a warm place until the rolls have almost doubled in size. Meanwhile, preheat the oven to 450°F. Brush the rolls lightly with melted butter to glaze. Bake for about 12–15 minutes or until lightly browned. Cool slightly on a wire rack before serving.

Quick Breads, Muffins & Cookies

Make snack time a memorable occasion with this irresistible collection of quick breads, muffins and cookies. Try the deliciously light Lemon and Walnut Loaf or savor the mouthwatering Dried Cherry Muffins. You're sure to delight everyone.

Lemon & Walnut Loaf

INGREDIENTS

½ cup butter or margarine, at
room temperature
½ cup sugar
2 eggs, separated
grated zest of 2 lemons
2 tablespoons lemon juice
2 cups all-purpose flour
2 teaspoons baking powder
½–⅔ cup milk
½ cup chopped walnuts
pinch of salt

MAKES I LOAF

1 Preheat the oven to 350°F. Grease a 1-pound loaf pan and line it with a sheet of baking parchment. Set aside.

2 Cream the butter or margarine with the sugar until light and fluffy. Beat in the egg yolks, then stir in the lemon zest and juice.

3 In another bowl, sift the flour and baking powder together three times. Fold into the creamed mixture in three batches, alternating with ½ cup of the milk. Fold in the walnuts. The mixture should be quite stiff; add the extra milk only if absolutely necessary.

4 Whisk the egg whites with the salt in a bowl until stiff. Fold half the egg white into the walnut mixture to lighten it, then fold in the rest until just mixed.

5 Spoon the mixture into the prepared pan. Bake for 45 minutes or until a thin skewer inserted in the teabread comes out clean. Cool on a wire rack.

36

Pineapple & Apricot Loaf

INGREDIENTS

2 cups flour
1/4 teaspoon salt
1 1/2 teaspoons baking powder
3/4 cup sweet butter
2/3 cup sugar
3 eggs, beaten
few drops of vanilla extract
2/3 cup crystalized pineapple, chopped
2/3 cup crystalized ginger, chopped
1 1/3 cups ready-to-eat dried apricots, chopped
grated zest and juice of 1/2 orange
grated zest and juice of 1/2 lemon
milk (see method)

MAKES 1 LOAF

37

1 Preheat the oven to 350°F. Line a 7-inch square loaf pan with wax paper. Grease the paper. Sift the flour, salt and baking powder into a bowl.

2 Cream the butter and sugar together in a mixing bowl until pale and fluffy. Gradually add the beaten eggs, beating well after each addition, and adding a little of the flour mixture if the mixture shows signs of curdling. Beat in the vanilla extract, then fold in half of the remaining flour mixture.

3 Fold in the pineapple, ginger, apricots and grated citrus zest, with the rest of the flour. Add enough of the citrus juice to give a fairly soft dropping consistency. (Add a little milk if necessary.) Spoon into the prepared pan, and level the top.

4 Bake for 20 minutes, then lower the oven temperature to 325°F, and bake for 1–1 1/4 hours more, until firm. Cool for 10 minutes in the pan, then turn out on a wire rack to cool.

Banana & Orange Loaf

INGREDIENTS

¾ cup whole-wheat flour
¾ cup flour
1 teaspoon baking powder
1 teaspoon ground cinnamon
3 tablespoons sliced hazelnuts, toasted
2 large, ripe bananas
1 egg
2 tablespoons sunflower oil
2 tablespoons clear honey
finely grated zest and juice of 1 small orange
DECORATION
4 orange slices, halved
2 teaspoons confectioners' sugar

MAKES 1 LOAF

I Preheat the oven to 350°F. Line the base of a 9 x 5-inch loaf pan with wax paper and grease the paper with a little oil. Sift the flours, baking powder and cinnamon together into a mixing bowl, adding any bran that remains in the sifter. Stir in the sliced hazelnuts. Mix until all ingredients are thoroughly combined.

2 Mash both of the bananas in a mixing bowl with a fork. Beat in the egg, sunflower oil, honey, orange zest and juice. Add to the dry ingredients, and mix well. Spoon the banana mixture into the prepared loaf pan, and smooth down the top with a knife or with the back of a spoon.

3 Bake for 40–45 minutes, or until firm and golden brown. Turn out on to a wire rack. Let cool until required. Preheat the broiler.

4 Sprinkle the orange slices with the confectioners' sugar. Place them on a rack over a broiler pan, and broil until golden, taking care not to let them burn. Cool slightly. Arrange the slices on top of the loaf.

COOK'S TIP
If you plan to keep the loaf for more than two to three days, omit the orange slices, and brush the warm loaf with honey instead. Sprinkle with sliced hazelnuts, if you like.

Banana & Cardamom Bread

INGREDIENTS

1½ cups milk
good pinch of saffron strands
2 tablespoons clear honey, plus extra
for glazing
2 ripe bananas
3 tablespoons sugar
8 cups white bread flour
1 teaspoon salt
2 tablespoons butter
2 x ¼-ounce sachets fast-rising
dried yeast
seeds from 6 cardamom pods
⅔ cup raisins

MAKES 2 LOAVES

1 Heat the milk in a saucepan to simmering point. Pour a little into a cup and crumble in the saffron strands. Set aside to infuse for 5 minutes. Stir the

honey into the remaining milk, pour into a pitcher and cool slightly. Using a fork, mash the bananas with the sugar.

2 Mix the flour and salt in a bowl. Rub in the butter until the mixture resembles breadcrumbs, then stir in the yeast and cardamom seeds.

3 Make a well in the center and strain in the saffron milk. Add the honey-flavored milk, mashed banana mixture and raisins. Mix to a soft dough. Add more hand-hot milk, if necessary.

4 Lightly grease two 1-pound loaf pans. Knead the dough on a lightly floured surface for 10 minutes. Divide the dough in half and fit each half into a loaf pan.

5 Slip the pans into a lightly oiled plastic bag and leave the loaves to rise for about 1½ hours until they have doubled in bulk. Preheat the oven to 400°F.

6 Bake the loaves for 20 minutes, then lower the oven temperature to 350°F and bake for 20–25 minutes more, or until they sound hollow when tapped underneath. Place on wire racks and brush the tops with honey while the loaves are still warm.

Raisin Bread

INGREDIENTS

1½ cups seedless raisins
1 tablespoon brandy
½ teaspoon grated nutmeg
grated zest of 1 large orange
½ cup butter
2 cups milk
6 cups all-purpose flour
1 teaspoon salt
6 tablespoons sugar
1 tablespoon fast-rising dried yeast
1 egg beaten with 1 tablespoon light cream,
for glazing

MAKES 2 LOAVES

42

1 Mix the raisins, brandy, nutmeg and orange zest in a bowl. Melt ¼ cup of the butter in the milk in a saucepan. Cool slightly.

2 Sift the flour into a large mixing bowl and stir in the salt, sugar and yeast. Add the milk mixture and mix to a dough, then knead on a lightly floured surface for 10 minutes, until smooth and elastic.

3 Grease two 1-pound loaf pans. Melt the remaining butter. Divide the dough in half. Roll each half into a rectangle measuring 20 x 8 inches.

4 Brush with the melted butter and sprinkle evenly with the raisin mixture. Roll up from a short side, tucking in the ends slightly. Place in the pans, cover and leave in a warm place to rise for about 1½ hours or until doubled in bulk. Preheat the oven to 400°F.

5 Glaze the loaves with the egg and cream mixture. Bake for 20 minutes, then lower the oven temperature to 350°F and bake for 20–25 minutes more, or until golden. Cool on wire racks.

Cranberry & Orange Bread

INGREDIENTS

2 cups all-purpose flour
2 teaspoons baking powder
½ cup sugar
½ teaspoon salt
grated zest of 1 large orange
¾ cup orange juice
2 eggs, lightly beaten
6 tablespoons butter, melted
1 cup fresh cranberries or
blueberries
½ cup chopped walnuts

MAKES 1 LOAF

1 Preheat the oven to 350°F. Grease a 1-pound loaf pan, line it with a sheet of baking parchment and set aside.

2 Sift the flour and baking powder into a mixing bowl. Stir in the sugar, salt and orange zest. Make a well in the center and add the orange juice, eggs and  melted butter. Stir from the center until the ingredients are just blended; do not overmix.

3 Add the berries and walnuts and stir gently until just mixed. Spread the mixture in the pan and bake for 45–50 minutes, until the loaf is golden and the surface  springs back when lightly touched with a finger.

4 Cool the bread in the pan for 10 minutes, then transfer to a wire rack to cool completely. Serve the bread thinly sliced, with butter or cream cheese and jam.

43

Swedish Golden Raisin Bread

INGREDIENTS

¾ cup milk
⅔ cup water
1 tablespoon clear honey
2 cups whole-wheat flour
2 cups white bread flour
1 teaspoon salt
2 teaspoons fast-rising dried yeast
⅔ cup golden raisins
½ cup chopped walnuts
milk, for glazing

MAKES 1 LOAF

44

1 Bring the milk and water to simmering point in a small saucepan. Stir in the honey until dissolved, then pour the milk mixture into a pitcher and leave to cool for a while.

2 Sift both kinds of flour into a mixing bowl. Stir in the salt, yeast and raisins. Set aside 1 tablespoon of the walnuts and add the rest to the bowl. Mix lightly. Make a well in the center of the dry ingredients.

3 Add the hand-hot liquid to the well and mix to a soft dough. Add a little extra hand-hot water if necessary. Knead the dough on a lightly floured surface for 10 minutes, making sure that the dried fruit and nuts are well distributed.

4 Lightly grease a cookie sheet. Pat the dough into an 11-inch long sausage and place it on the cookie sheet. Make about four diagonal cuts down the length.

5 Slide the cookie sheet into a lightly oiled plastic bag. Leave the bread to rise in a warm place for about 1½ hours. Preheat the oven to 425°F.

6 Brush the dough with milk, sprinkle it with the reserved walnuts and bake for about 10 minutes. Lower the oven temperature to 400°F and bake for 20 minutes more. Cool on a wire rack.

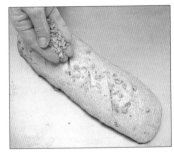

Braided Prune Bread

INGREDIENTS

¼ cup butter
4 tablespoons milk
4 cups all-purpose flour
½ teaspoon salt
¼ cup sugar
¼-ounce sachet fast-rising dried yeast
1 egg, lightly beaten
4 tablespoon hand-hot water
1 egg, beaten with 2 teaspoons
water, for glazing
FILLING
generous 1 cup cooked pitted prunes
2 teaspoons grated lemon zest
1 teaspoon grated orange zest
¼ teaspoon grated nutmeg
3 tbsp butter, melted
½ cup walnuts, very finely chopped
2 tablespoons sugar

MAKES 1 LOAF

1 Melt the butter in the milk in a saucepan. Pour into a small pitcher and cool slightly. Sift the flour into a large mixing bowl and stir in the salt, sugar and yeast.

2 Make a well in the center of the dry ingredients and add the milk mixture with the beaten egg. Mix in enough of the hand-hot water to make a soft dough. Knead on a lightly floured surface for about 10 minutes, until the dough is smooth and elastic. Return the dough to the clean bowl, cover with a dish cloth and leave in a warm place to rise for about 1½ hours or until doubled in bulk.

3 Lightly grease a large cookie sheet. Make the filling by mixing all the ingredients in a bowl. When the dough is ready, punch it down, then roll it out on a lightly floured surface to a rectangle measuring 15 x 10 inches. Transfer to the cookie sheet.

4 Spread the filling in the center of the dough. Cut strips at an angle on either side of the filling, fold up one end neatly, then bring alternate strips up over the filling to make the braid. Tuck the excess dough underneath at the ends, to neaten.

5 Cover the braid loosely and leave in a warm place to rise again. Preheat the oven to 375°F. Glaze the braid with the egg wash and bake for 30 minutes or until golden. Cool on a wire rack.

Apricot Nut Loaf

INGREDIENTS

⅔ cup dried apricots
1 large orange
½ cup raisins
⅔ cup sugar
6 tablespoons sunflower oil
2 eggs, lightly beaten
2¼ cups flour
2 teaspoons baking powder
½ teaspoon salt
1 teaspoon baking soda
½ cup chopped walnuts
butter, to serve

MAKES I LOAF

1 Line a 9 x 5-inch loaf pan with wax paper. Grease the paper well. Place the dried apricots in a bowl, and cover with warm water. Then let stand for about 30 minutes.

2 Preheat the oven to 350°F. Remove the orange zest carefully, and cut the zest into thin matchsticks. Squeeze the orange, and add water to the juice, if necessary, to make ¾ cup liquid.

3 Drain the apricots, and cut into small pieces. Mix the orange zest, apricots and raisins in a bowl, and pour over the orange juice. Mix together well. Stir in the sugar, oil and eggs.

4 In a separate bowl, sift together the flour, baking powder, salt and the baking soda. Fold this into the apricot mixture in three batches. Stir in the walnuts.

5 Spoon the mixture into the prepared pan, and bake for 55–60 minutes or until a cake tester inserted in the loaf comes out clean. Let cool in the pan for 10 minutes, then transfer to a rack. Let cool completely before serving with butter.

Date & Pecan Loaf

INGREDIENTS

1 cup pitted dates, chopped
¾ cup boiling water
1½ cups all-purpose flour
2 teaspoons salt
2 teapsoons baking powder
½ teaspoon salt
¼ teaspoon grated nutmeg
¼ cup butter, at room
temperature
⅓ cup dark brown sugar
¼ cup sugar
1 egg, lightly beaten
2 tablespoons brandy
¾ cup chopped pecan nuts

MAKES 1 LOAF

2 Sift the flour, baking powder and salt together. Add the nutmeg. Cream the butter with the sugars in a mixing bowl until light and fluffy. Beat in the egg and brandy.

3 Fold the dry ingredients into the creamed mixture in three batches, alternating with the dates (and soaking water).

4 Fold the chopped pecans into the mixture, scrape it into the pan and level the surface. Bake for 45–50 minutes or until a skewer inserted in the loaf comes out clean. Cool in the pan for 10 minutes before transferring to a wire rack to cool completely.

49

1 Place the dates in a heatproof bowl and pour over the boiling water. Set aside to cool. Meanwhile preheat the oven to 350°F. Then grease a 1-pound

loaf pan, line with a sheet of baking parchment and set aside.

Malt Loaf

INGREDIENTS

⅔ cup milk
3 tablespoons malt extract
3 cups all-purpose flour
½ teaspoon salt
¼-ounce sachet fast-rising dried yeast
2 tablespoons light muscovado sugar
1 cup golden raisins
1 tablespoon sunflower oil
GLAZE
2 tablespoons sugar
2 tablespoons water

MAKES 1 LOAF

1 Grease a 1-pound loaf pan. Heat the milk in a saucepan to simmering point. Stir in the malt extract until dissolved. Set aside to cool slightly.

2 Mix the flour, salt, yeast and sugar in a bowl. Stir in the raisins. Make a well in the center and add the milk mixture and oil. Mix to a soft dough,  adding more hand-hot milk if necessary.

3 Knead the dough on a lightly floured surface for 10 minutes, until smooth and elastic. Fit it in the loaf pan, cover and leave in a warm place to rise  for about 1½ hours until it has doubled in bulk. Preheat the oven to 375°F.

4 Bake the loaf for 30 minutes, until it sounds hollow when tapped underneath. Meanwhile make the glaze. Dissolve the sugar in the water in a small pan. Bring to a boil, stirring, then lower the heat and simmer for 1 minute.

5 Put the loaf on a wire rack and brush it with the glaze while still hot. Leave the loaf to cool. Serve with butter and jam, if liked.

Dried Cherry Muffins

52

INGREDIENTS

1 cup plain yogurt
1 cup dried cherries
½ cup butter, at room temperature
¾ cup sugar
2 eggs
1 teaspoon vanilla extract
1¾ cups flour
2 teaspoons baking powder
1 teaspoon baking soda
pinch of salt

MAKES 16

1 In a mixing bowl, combine the yogurt and cherries. Cover, and let stand for 30 minutes.

2 Preheat the oven to 350°F. Grease a 16-cup muffin pan, or arrange 16 double paper cupcake cases on cookie sheets.

3 With an electric mixer, cream the butter and sugar together until light and fluffy.

4 Add the eggs, one at a time, beating well after each addition. Add the vanilla extract and the cherry mixture. Stir to blend, and set aside.

5 In another bowl, sift together the flour, baking powder, baking soda and salt. Carefully fold into the cherry mixture in three batches.

6 Fill the cases or muffin pan two-thirds full. Bake for about 20 minutes, until the tops spring back when touched lightly. Transfer to a wire rack to cool.

Chocolate Chip Muffins

INGREDIENTS

1/2 cup sweet butter or margarine
generous 1/4 cup superfine sugar
2 tablespoons dark brown sugar
2 eggs, beaten
1 1/2 cups flour
1 teaspoon baking powder
1/2 cup milk
1 cup semisweet chocolate chips

MAKES 10

3 Divide half the mixture between ten muffin cups or cases, and sprinkle the chocolate chips over. Then cover with the remaining mixture. Bake for 20–25 minutes, or until the muffins are well risen. The tops of the muffins should spring back when lightly touched. If paper cases were not used, cool in the cups for 5 minutes before turning out. Serve warm or cold.

1 Preheat the oven to 375°F. Lightly grease a 12-cup muffin pan, or use large paper cupcake cups. With an electric mixer, beat the sweet butter or margarine with the superfine and dark brown sugar until light and fluffy. Beat in the eggs, a little at a time, adding a small amount of flour if the mixture shows any signs of curdling.

2 Sift the flour and baking powder into a separate bowl. Fold into the creamed mixture in stages, alternately with the milk.

Apple & Cranberry Muffins

INGREDIENTS

1¼ cups flour
1 teaspoon baking powder
½ teaspoon baking soda
1 teaspoon ground cinnamon
½ teaspoon grated nutmeg
½ teaspoon ground allspice
¼ teaspoon ground ginger
¼ teaspoon salt
¼ cup sweet butter or margarine
1 egg, beaten
6 tablespoons sugar
grated zest of 1 large orange
½ cup freshly squeezed orange juice
1–2 eating apples
1 cup cranberries
½ cup chopped walnuts
confectioners' sugar, for dusting

MAKES 12

1 Preheat the oven to 350°F. Lightly grease a 12-cup muffin pan. Sift the flour, baking powder, baking soda, ground spices and salt into a large bowl. Melt the butter or margarine.

2 Whisk together the beaten egg and melted butter or margarine. Add the sugar, orange zest and juice, and mix together well.

3 Peel, quarter, and core the apples, then chop coarsely. Make a well in the center of the dry ingredients, and pour in the egg mixture. With a large metal spoon, stir for just long enough to moisten the flour—the mixture need not be smooth.

4 Fold the apples, cranberries and walnuts into the mixture. Spoon the mixture into the muffin cups, filling them three-quarters full. Bake for 25–30 minutes until the muffins are well risen. The tops should spring back when lightly touched. Cool in the cups for 5 minutes before turning out. Serve warm or cold, dusted with confectioners' sugar.

Chocolate Nut Cookies

INGREDIENTS

1 ounce semisweet chocolate, broken into squares
1 ounce bittersweet cooking chocolate,
broken into squares
2 cups flour
1/2 teaspoon salt
1 cup sweet butter, at room temperature
1 cup sugar
2 eggs, beaten
1 teaspoon vanilla extract
1 cup walnuts, finely chopped

MAKES 50

56

1 Combine the chocolate squares in a heatproof bowl. Bring a small saucepan of water to a boil, remove from the heat, and place the bowl on top. Set aside until the chocolate has completely melted, then stir until smooth. Sift the flour and salt into a small bowl, and set aside.

2 Using an electric mixer, cream the butter in a mixing bowl until soft. Add the sugar, and beat until light and fluffy. Beat in the eggs and vanilla extract, a little at a time. Then stir in the melted chocolate. Add the flour mixture and the nuts, and fold in gently until well mixed together.

3 Divide the mixture equally into four parts, and, with your hands, roll each into a log, about 2 inches in diameter. Wrap each of the chocolate logs tightly in foil, and refrigerate overnight, or place the logs in the freezer for several hours until firm.

4 Preheat the oven to 375°F. Grease two or three cookie sheets. With a sharp knife, cut the logs into 1/4-inch slices. Place the rounds on the cookie sheets, and bake for 10 minutes or until lightly colored. Cool on wire racks.

Chocolate-tipped Hazelnut Crescents

INGREDIENTS

2 cups flour
pinch of salt
1 cup sweet butter, softened
¼ cup sugar
1 tablespoon hazelnut liqueur or water
1 teaspoon vanilla extract
1 pound semisweet chocolate
½ cup roasted chopped hazelnuts
confectioners' sugar, for dusting

MAKES ABOUT 35

1 Preheat the oven to 325°F. Grease two large cookie sheets. Sift the flour and salt together into a bowl, and set aside.

2 Using an electric mixer, cream the butter in a mixing bowl. Add the sugar, and beat until fluffy. Then beat in the hazelnut liqueur or water and vanilla extract. Gently stir in the flour mixture, until just blended. Set aside 12 ounces of the chocolate, and grate the rest into the mixture. Add the chopped hazelnuts, and fold in lightly.

3 With very lightly floured hands, carefully shape the dough into about 35 2 x ½-inch crescents. Place, about 2–3 inches apart, on the cookie sheets, then  bake for 20–25 minutes until golden. Cool on the cookie sheets for 10 minutes, then use a spatula to transfer to wire racks to cool completely.

4 Line the clean cookie sheets with nonstick parchment paper. Dust the crescents with confectioners' sugar. Melt the remaining chocolate in a bowl over hot water. Using tongs, dip half of each crescent into the chocolate. Place on the prepared cookie sheets, and refrigerate until the chocolate has set.

Apricot Yogurt Cookies

INGREDIENTS

1 1/2 cups flour
1 teaspoon baking powder
1 teaspoon ground cinnamon
1 cup rolled oats
1/2 cup light brown sugar
2/3 cup ready-to-eat dried apricots
1 tablespoon sliced hazelnuts or almonds
2/3 cup plain yogurt, plus extra yogurt
or milk (see method)
3 tablespoons sunflower oil
raw sugar, to sprinkle

MAKES 16

I Preheat the oven to 375°F. Lightly grease a large cookie sheet with oil. Sift together the flour, baking powder and cinnamon into a large mixing bowl. Using a wooden spoon, stir in the oats, light brown sugar, dried apricots and nuts.

2 In a small bowl, whisk the yogurt and oil together. Pour into the flour mixture, and mix to a firm dough. If necessary, add a little extra yogurt or milk.

3 With floured hands, form the mixture into 16 rough mounds. Place them on the cookie sheet, leaving room for spreading, then flatten with a fork. Sprinkle with sugar, and bake for 15–20 minutes. Cool for 5 minutes, then transfer to a wire rack.

COOK'S TIP

These cookies do not keep very well, so it is best to eat them within two days, or freeze them. Pack in plastic bags, label, and freeze them for up to four months.

Savory Pies

Everyone loves delicious savory pies. From the traditional British Steak, Kidney & Mushroom to the succulent Salmon and Ginger with Lemon Thyme & Lime, there's sure to be a pie here to suit every occasion.

Old-fashioned Chicken Pie

INGREDIENTS

1 chicken, about 4–4½ pounds
1 onion, quartered
1 tarragon or rosemary sprig
1¼ cups water
2 tablespoons butter
1 cup small button mushrooms
2 tablespoons flour
4 ounces cooked ham, diced
2 tablespoons chopped fresh parsley
1 pound fresh or thawed frozen puff pastry
1 egg, beaten
salt and ground black pepper

SERVES 4

1 Preheat the oven to 400°F. Put the chicken in a casserole, with the onion, herb sprig and water. Cover with a lid, and bake for 1¼ hours or until the meat is tender.

2 Transfer the chicken to a plate, and remove the skin. Strain the cooking liquid into a pitcher or bowl. Set aside to cool. Remove the meat from the chicken bones, cutting it into large chunks.

3 Melt the butter in a saucepan. Cook the mushrooms for 2–3 minutes. Meanwhile skim off any fat from the surface of the chicken stock. Add water to make the stock up to 1¼ cups.

4 Sprinkle flour over the button mushrooms, then gradually stir in the chicken stock. Bring to a boil, stirring, then add the ham, chicken and parsley, with salt and pepper to taste. Turn into one large or four individual pie dishes, and set aside to cool.

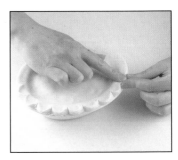

5 Roll out the pastry on a lightly floured surface to a round or oval about 2 inches larger than the pie dish. Cut a narrow strip to place around the edge of the dish, brush it lightly with beaten egg, then fit the lid in place. Scallop the edges, and knock up the sides with the back of a knife. Cut a hole in the center of the pie(s) to allow the steam to escape. Decorate with pastry leaves.

6 Heat the oven to 400°F again. Glaze the pastry with beaten egg. Bake until well risen and golden brown. Individual pies will require 25–35 minutes and a large pie 35–45 minutes.

Pennsylvania Dutch Ham & Apple Pie

INGREDIENTS

2 cups all-purpose flour
½ teaspoon salt
6 tablespoons cold butter
4 tablespoons cold margarine
¼–½ cup ice water
FILLING
5 cooking apples
4 tablespoons light brown sugar
1 tablespoon flour
¾ teaspoon ground cloves
¾ teaspoon ground black pepper
6 ounces sliced baked ham
2 tablespoons butter or margarine
4 tablespoons whipping cream
1 egg yolk

SERVES 6–8

68

1 To make the crust, sift the flour and salt into a bowl. Rub in the butter and margarine until the mixture resembles coarse crumbs. Stir in enough water to bind, gather the dough into two balls, and wrap in plastic wrap. Chill for 20 minutes. Preheat the oven to 425°F.

2 Quarter, core, peel, and thinly slice the apples. Place in a bowl and toss with the sugar, flour, cloves and pepper, to coat evenly. Set aside.

3 Roll out one dough ball ⅛ inch thick. Fit in a 10-inch pie dish. Leave an overhang.

4 Arrange half the ham slices in the bottom. Top with a layer of apple slices. Dot with half the butter or margarine. Repeat layering, finishing with apples. Dot with butter or margarine. Pour 3 tablespoons of the whipping cream on top, in an even layer.

5 Roll out the remaining dough and put it on top of the pie. Fold the top edge under the bottom crust and press to seal. Roll out the dough scraps and stamp out decorative shapes. Arrange on top of the pie. Crimp the edge using your finger and a fork. Cut steam vents at regular intervals. Mix the egg yolk and remaining cream and brush on top of the pie to glaze. Avoid clogging the steam vents.

6 Bake for about 10 minutes. Reduce the heat to 350°F. Bake for 30–35 minutes more, until golden. Serve hot.

Bacon & Egg Pie

INGREDIENTS

1–1¼ pounds shortcrust pastry, thawed
if frozen
2 tablespoons oil
4 strips bacon, cut into
1-inch pieces
1 small onion, finely chopped
5 eggs
1½ tablespoons chopped fresh
parsley (optional)
salt and ground black pepper
beaten egg or milk, to glaze

SERVES 4

70

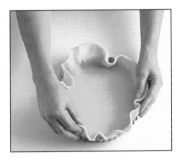

1 Use two-thirds of the pastry to line an 8-inch quiche pan. Chill for 20 minutes. Preheat the oven to 400°F. Heat the oil in a pan and fry the bacon and onion until the onion is soft, and the bacon is starting to crisp. Drain on paper towels.

2 Cover the bottom of the pastry with the bacon mixture, spreading it evenly, then break the eggs over the bacon, spacing them evenly apart. Carefully tilt the quiche pan so the egg whites flow together. Sprinkle the eggs with the chopped fresh parsley, if using, plenty of black pepper, and salt—just a little if the bacon is very salty. Place a baking sheet in the oven to heat.

3 Roll out the remaining pastry, dampen the edges and place over the filling. Press to seal the edges, then remove excess pastry and use for pastry leaves. Decorate the pie, brush it with egg or milk and make a hole in the center.

4 Place the pie on the baking sheet and bake for 10 minutes, then reduce the oven temperature to 350°F and bake for 20 minutes. Let cool before cutting.

Greek Lamb Pie

INGREDIENTS

sunflower oil, for brushing
1 pound lean ground lamb
1 medium onion, sliced
1 garlic clove, crushed
14-ounce can plum tomatoes
2 tablespoons chopped fresh mint
1 teaspoon grated nutmeg
12 ounces young spinach leaves
10-ounce package phyllo pastry
1 teaspoon sesame seeds
salt and ground black pepper

SERVES 4

4 Lightly brush each sheet of phyllo pastry with oil and lay in overlapping layers in the pan, leaving enough overhanging to wrap over the top.

5 Spoon in the meat and spinach. Wrap the pastry over to enclose the filling; scrunch it slightly. Sprinkle with sesame seeds and bake the pie for 25–30 minutes, or until golden and crisp. Serve the pie hot, using a sharp knife to cut through the phyllo.

1 Preheat the oven to 400°F. Lightly oil a 9-inch round springform pan.

2 Fry the lamb and onion without fat in a non-stick pan until golden. Add the garlic, tomatoes, mint, nutmeg, salt and pepper. Bring to a boil, stirring. Simmer, stirring occasionally, until most of the liquid has evaporated.

3 Wash the spinach and remove any tough stalks. Place the wet leaves in a saucepan, cover and cook for about 2 minutes, until wilted.

Lamb Pie with Pear & Mint Sauce

INGREDIENTS

*1 boned mid-loin of lamb, about 2¼ pounds
after boning
1 tablespoon oil
2 tablespoons butter, plus extra for greasing
8 large sheets phyllo pastry
salt and ground black pepper
Italian parsley, to garnish*
STUFFING & SAUCE
*1 small onion, chopped
1 tablespoon butter
1 cup whole-wheat bread crumbs
grated zest of 1 lemon
¼ teaspoon ground ginger
14-ounce can pears
1 egg, beaten
2 teaspoons finely chopped fresh mint, plus
a small sprig, to garnish*

SERVES 6

1 Make the stuffing. Fry the onion in the butter until soft. Pour into a bowl, and add the bread crumbs, lemon zest and ginger. Drain the pears, reserving the juice and half the fruit. Chop the remaining pears, and add them to the mixture. Season, and bind with the egg. Spread the loin out flat, fat-side down, and season. Place the stuffing along the middle of the loin, and roll up carefully.

2 Holding the meat firmly, close the opening with a trussing needle threaded with string. Heat the oil in a heavy-based frying pan, and brown the roll slowly on all sides, until well colored. Let cool, and store in the fridge until needed.

3 Preheat the oven to 400°F. Melt the butter. Keeping the remainder of the phyllo covered, brush two sheets with a little butter. Overlap by about 5 inches to make a square. Place the next two sheets on top, and brush with butter. Continue until all the phyllo has been used.

4 Remove the string from the lamb, and place the roll diagonally across one corner of the pastry, so that it sits within the pastry square, without over-hanging the edges. Fold the corner of the pastry over the lamb, fold in the sides, and brush with melted butter. Roll up neatly. Place the roll join-side down on a greased baking sheet, and bake for 40 minutes, covering it with foil if it browns too rapidly and looks as if it might burn.

5 Meanwhile, make the sauce. Purée the reserved pears, juice and mint. Pour into a sauce-boat, and garnish with a mint sprig. Place the lamb on a platter, garnish with Italian parsley, and serve with the pear and mint sauce.

72

Mixed Game Pie

INGREDIENTS

*1 pound game meat, off the bone, diced
(plus the carcasses and bones)
1 small onion, halved
2 bay leaves
2 carrots, halved
a few black peppercorns
1 tablespoon oil
½ cup chopped lean bacon
1 tablespoon flour
3 tablespoons sweet sherry or Madeira
2 teaspoons ground ginger
grated zest and juice of ½ orange
12 ounces puff pastry, thawed if frozen
salt and ground black pepper
beaten egg or milk, to glaze
red currant or apple jelly, to serve*

SERVES 4

1 Place the carcasses and bones in a pan, with any giblets and half the onion, the bay leaves, carrots and peppercorns. Cover with water and bring to a boil. Simmer until reduced to about 1¼ cups, then strain the stock into a bowl.

2 Chop the other onion half and fry in the oil until soft. Add the bacon and meat and fry quickly to seal. Sprinkle on the flour and stir until beginning to brown. Gradually add the stock, stirring constantly as it thickens, then add the sherry or Madeira, ground ginger, orange zest and juice, and salt and pepper. Simmer for 20 minutes, until thick and flavorful. Check the seasoning.

3 Transfer to a 4-cup pie dish and allow to cool slightly. Put a pie funnel in the center of the filling to help hold up the pastry.

4 Preheat the oven to 425°F. Roll out the pastry to 1 inch larger than the dish. Cut off a ½-inch strip all around. Moisten the rim of the dish and press on the strip of pastry. Dampen the pastry strip, then lift the pastry lid carefully over the pie, sealing the edges at the rim. Trim off the excess pastry and scallop the edge. Decorate the top, then brush the pie with egg or milk to glaze.

5 Bake for 15 minutes, then reduce the heat to 375°F and bake for 25–30 more minutes. Serve with red currant or apple jelly.

Steak, Kidney & Mushroom Pie

INGREDIENTS

2 tablespoons oil
1 onion, chopped
4 ounces lean bacon, chopped
1¼ pounds chuck steak, diced
2 tablespoons flour
4 ounces lamb's kidneys
large bouquet garni
1¾ cups beef stock
1½ cups button mushrooms
8 ounces puff pastry, thawed if frozen
salt and ground black pepper
beaten egg, to glaze

SERVES 4

1 Preheat the oven to 325°F. Heat the oil in a heavy frying pan, then cook the onion and bacon until lightly browned.

2 Toss the steak in the flour. Stir the meat into the pan in batches and cook, stirring, until browned.

3 Toss the kidneys in flour and add to the pan with the bouquet garni. Pour in the stock, transfer to a casserole, put on the lid and cook in the oven for 2 hours. Stir in the mushrooms and seasoning and set the casserole aside to cool completely.

4 Preheat the oven to 425°F. Roll out the pastry to ¾ inch larger than the top of a 5-cup pie dish. Cut off a narrow strip from the pastry and fit it around the dampened rim of the dish. Brush the pastry strip with water.

5 Pour the meat mixture into the dish. Lay the pastry over the dish, press the edges to seal, then crimp them decoratively with the back of a knife. Make a small slit in the pastry, brush with beaten egg and bake for 20 minutes. Reduce the oven temperature to 350°F and bake for 20 minutes longer, until the pastry is golden.

Golden Fish Pie

INGREDIENTS

1½ pounds white fish fillets
1¼ cups milk
black peppercorns, bay leaf and onion slices,
to flavor
4 ounces cooked, peeled shrimp, thawed
if frozen
½ cup butter
½ cup all-purpose flour
1¼ cups light cream
¾ cup grated Gruyère cheese
1 bunch watercress, leaves only, chopped
1 teaspoon Dijon mustard
5 sheets phyllo pastry
salt and ground black pepper

SERVES 4–6

1 Place the fish fillets in a pan, pour on the milk and add the flavoring ingredients. Bring just to a boil, then cover and simmer for 10–12 minutes, until the fish is just cooked through. Watch the pan closely, as milk boils over easily.

2 Lift out the fish, remove the skin and bones, then flake it into a shallow ovenproof dish. Scatter the shrimp on top. Strain the milk and reserve.

3 Melt 4 tablespoons of the butter in a pan. Stir in the flour and cook for 1 minute. Stir in the reserved milk and cream. Bring to a boil, stirring, then simmer for 2–3 minutes, still stirring, until the sauce has thickened and is rich and creamy.

4 Remove the pan from the heat and stir in the Gruyère, watercress, mustard and seasoning to taste. Pour the sauce over the fish and let cool.

5 Preheat the oven to 375°F. Melt the rest of the butter. Brush one sheet of phyllo pastry with melted butter. Crumple it loosely and place gently on top of the fish filling. Repeat with the rest of the phyllo sheets and butter, until they are all used up and the pie is completely covered.

6 Bake in the oven for 25–30 minutes, until the phyllo pastry is golden and crisp, and the filling is piping hot. Serve the pie immediately. Use a large, very sharp knife to cut the pie.

78

Salmon & Ginger Pie, with Lemon Thyme & Lime

INGREDIENTS

1 salmon fillet (1¾ pounds)
3 tablespoons walnut oil
1 tablespoon fresh lime juice
2 teaspoons chopped fresh lemon thyme,
plus extra sprigs to garnish
2 tablespoons white wine
14-ounce package puff pastry,
thawed if frozen
½ cup slivered almonds
3–4 pieces preserved ginger in syrup,
drained and chopped
salt and ground black pepper
beaten egg, to glaze

SERVES 4–6

I Split the salmon in half, remove the bones and skin, and divide into four fillets. Mix the oil, lime juice, thyme, wine and pepper to taste, and pour over the fish in a shallow dish. Cover tightly and let the salmon marinate overnight in the fridge.

2 Divide the pastry into two pieces, one slightly larger than the other, and roll out—the smaller piece should be large enough to hold two of the salmon fillets side by side and the second piece about 2 inches larger all around. Drain the fillets and discard the marinade.

3 Preheat the oven to 350°F. Place the smaller piece of pastry on a baking sheet, then arrange two of the fillets on top. Season. Sprinkle the fish with the almonds, ginger and a little more lemon thyme, if desired. Cover these fillets with the other two salmon fillets.

4 Season again, cover with the second piece of pastry, tuck the edges under the pastry base and seal well. Brush with beaten egg and decorate with any leftover pastry. Bake for 40 minutes until the crust is golden. Serve on a bed of lemon thyme.

Chestnut & Vegetable Pie

INGREDIENTS

1 pound puff pastry, thawed if frozen
1 pound Brussels sprouts, trimmed
3 tablespoons sunflower oil
1 large red bell pepper, sliced
1 large onion, sliced
about 16 whole chestnuts, peeled if fresh
1 egg yolk, beaten with 1 tablespoon water
SAUCE
scant ½ cup all-purpose flour
3 tablespoons butter
1¼ cups milk
¾ cup grated Cheddar cheese
2 tablespoons dry sherry
generous pinch of dried sage
3 tablespoons chopped fresh parsley
salt and ground black pepper

SERVES 6

1 Roll out the pastry to make two large rectangles, roughly the size of a large pie dish. The pastry should be about ¼ inch thick, and one rectangle should be slightly larger than the other. Set the pastry aside in the refrigerator to rest.

2 Blanch the Brussels sprouts for 4 minutes in 1¼ cups boiling water, then drain, reserving the water. Refresh the sprouts under cold running water, drain and set aside.

3 Heat the oil in a frying pan and lightly fry the red bell pepper and onion for 5 minutes. Set the pan aside. Cut each chestnut in half.

4 Make the sauce by beating the flour, butter and milk together over medium heat. Beat the sauce constantly as it comes to a boil, then stir until it is thickened and smooth. Stir in the reserved sprout water and the cheese, sherry, sage and seasoning. Simmer for 3 minutes to reduce, then stir in the chopped fresh parsley.

5 Fit the larger piece of pastry into your pie dish and layer the sprouts, chestnuts, pepper and onions on top. Trickle the sauce over the top, making sure it  seeps through to moisten the vegetables. Brush the pastry edges with the beaten egg yolk and water and fit the second pastry sheet on top, pressing the edges well to seal them securely.

6 Trim and crimp the edges, then slash the center several times. Glaze with the egg yolk. Set aside to rest somewhere cool while you preheat the oven to 400°F. Bake for about 30–40 minutes, until golden brown and crisp.

82

Green Lentil Phyllo Pie

INGREDIENTS

*1 cup green lentils, soaked for
30 minutes in water to cover, drained
2 bay leaves
2 onions, sliced
5 cups chicken or vegetable stock
¾ cup butter, melted
1¼ cups long-grain rice,
preferably basmati
4 tablespoons chopped fresh parsley, plus
a few sprigs to garnish
2 tablespoons chopped fresh dill
1 egg, beaten
2 cups mushrooms, sliced
about 8 sheets phyllo pastry
3 eggs, hard-cooked and sliced
salt and ground black pepper*

SERVES 6

1 Cover the lentils with water, then simmer with the bay leaves, one onion and half the stock for 20–25 minutes, or until tender. Season well. Set aside to cool.

2 Gently fry the remaining onion in another saucepan in 2 tablespoons of the butter, for 5 minutes. Stir in the rice and the rest of the stock. Season, bring to a boil, then cover and simmer for 12 minutes for basmati, 15 minutes for long grain. Let stand, uncovered, for 5 minutes, then stir in the fresh herbs and the beaten egg.

3 Fry the mushrooms in 3 tablespoons of the butter for 5 minutes, until they are just soft. Set aside to cool. Preheat the oven to 375°F.

4 Brush a large, shallow ovenproof dish with more butter. Lay the sheets of phyllo in it, covering the base but making sure most of the phyllo hangs over the sides. Brush the sheets of phyllo well with butter as you work, and overlap the pastry as required. Make sure there is a lot of pastry to fold over the green lentil filling.

5 Layer rice, lentils and mushrooms in the pastry shell, repeating the layers at least once and tucking the sliced egg in between. Season as you layer and form an even mound of filling. Bring up the sheets of pastry over the filling, scrunching the top into attractive folds. Brush all over with the rest of the butter and set aside to chill.

6 Bake the pie for about 45 minutes, until golden and crisp. Allow it to stand for 10 minutes before serving, garnished with parsley.

Curried Parsnip Pie

INGREDIENTS

½ cup butter
2 cups all-purpose flour
1 teaspoon dried thyme or oregano
cold water, to mix
1 egg yolk, beaten with 2 teaspoons water
FILLING
8 baby onions, peeled
2 carrots, thinly sliced
2 large parsnips, thinly sliced
2 tablespoons butter
2 tablespoons whole-wheat flour
1 tablespoon mild curry or tikka paste
1¼ cups milk
1 cup grated aged Cheddar cheese
3 tablespoons chopped fresh cilantro
salt and ground black pepper
cilantro or parsley sprig, to garnish

SERVES 4

1 Make the pastry. Rub the butter into the flour until it resembles coarse bread crumbs. Season well and stir in the thyme or oregano, then mix to a firm dough with cold water. Chill until needed.

2 Bring a pot of salted water to a boil, add the onions, carrots and parsnips, and boil for 5 minutes. Drain, reserving 1¼ cups of the cooking liquid.

3 Preheat the oven to 400°F. Melt the butter, stir in the flour and spice paste, then gradually whisk in the reserved liquid and milk, until thick and smooth. Stir in the cheese and seasoning, then add the vegetables and the cilantro. Pour into a pie pan, put a pie funnel in the center and allow to cool.

4 Roll out the pastry to ¾ inch larger than the top of the pie pan. Cut off a narrow strip from the pastry, brush with the egg yolk wash and place around the rim of the dish. Brush again with egg yolk wash. Using a rolling pin, lift the rolled-out pastry over the top of the pie and fit over the funnel, pressing it firmly onto the strips underneath. Trim the overhanging pastry and crimp the edges. Cut a hole for the funnel, decorate with pastry leaves and brush all over with the remaining egg yolk wash.

5 Bake the pie for 25–30 minutes until golden brown and crisp. Serve, garnished with a cilantro or parsley sprig.

Spinach & Feta Pie

INGREDIENTS

2 pounds fresh spinach, chopped
2 tablespoons butter or margarine
2 onions, chopped
2 garlic cloves, crushed
10 ounces feta cheese, crumbled
⅔ cup pine nuts
5 eggs, beaten
*2 saffron strands, soaked in 2 teaspoons
boiling water*
1 teaspoon paprika
¼ teaspoon ground cumin
¼ teaspoon ground cinnamon
14 sheets phyllo pastry
4 tablespoons olive oil
salt and ground black pepper
Romaine lettuce leaves, to serve

SERVES 6

1 Place the spinach in a large strainer, sprinkle with a little salt, rub it in and let drain for 30 minutes.

2 Preheat the oven to 350°F. Melt the butter or margarine in a large pan and fry the onions until golden. Add the garlic, cheese and pine nuts. Remove from the heat and stir in the eggs, spinach, saffron and spices. Season with salt and pepper and mix well. Set the mixture aside.

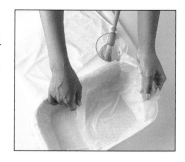

3 Grease a large rectangular baking dish. Take seven of the phyllo sheets and brush one side of each with a little olive oil. Place in the dish, overlapping the sheets so that the bottom is covered. Leave plenty of overhang to cover the filling later.

4 Spoon all the spinach mixture into the dish and carefully drizzle 2 tablespoons of the remaining olive oil over the top. Fold the overhanging pastry over the filling. Cut the remaining pastry sheets to the size of the dish and brush each one with more olive oil. Arrange on top of the filling.

5 Brush with water to prevent curling, then bake the pie for about 30 minutes, until the pastry is golden brown. Serve warm or cold, with a salad of crisp Romaine lettuce leaves.

COOK'S TIP
Cheddar, Parmesan or any hard cheese can be added to this dish with or in place of the feta.

88

Sweet Pies

For the perfect end to any meal choose from childhood favorites such as Open Apple Pie and Cherry Lattice Pie. Or, for an unforgettable finale, indulge in the velvety-smooth richness of a Chocolate Cheesecake Pie.

Plum Pie

INGREDIENTS

2½ cups flour
1 teaspoon salt
⅓ cup refrigerated sweet butter
½ cup refrigerated shortening
4–8 tablespoons iced water
milk, for glazing
FILLING
2 pounds red or purple plums, halved and pitted
grated zest of 1 lemon
1 tablespoon lemon juice
½–¾ cup sugar
3 tablespoons quick-cooking tapioca
pinch of salt
½ teaspoon ground cinnamon
¼ teaspoon grated nutmeg

SERVES 8

3 Roll out the smaller piece of pastry to a round slightly larger than the top of the pie. Support it on the prepared cookie sheet, then stamp out four hearts from the center of the pastry, using a cutter. Reserve the pastry hearts.

1 Sift the flour and salt into a bowl. Rub in the butter and shortening until the mixture resembles bread crumbs. Stir in just enough iced water to bind the pastry. Gather into two balls, one slightly larger than the other. Wrap, and refrigerate for 20 minutes.

4 Make the filling by mixing all the ingredients in a bowl. Use the larger quantity of sugar if the plums are very tart. Spoon the filling into the pastry shell, then lift the pastry on the wax paper, and slide it into position over the filling. Trim, and pinch to seal. Arrange the cut-out pastry hearts on top. Glaze the top of the pie with milk, and bake for 15 minutes. Lower the oven temperature to 350°F, and bake for 30–35 minutes more, protecting the top with foil if needed.

2 Preheat the oven to 425°F. Line a cookie sheet with wax paper. Set it aside. Roll out the larger piece of pastry to a thickness of about ⅛ inch, and line a 9-inch pie pan.

Walnut & Pear Lattice Pie

INGREDIENTS

2 cups flour
¼ teaspoon salt
½ cup refrigerated butter, diced
¼ cup finely chopped walnuts
3—4 tablespoons iced water
⅓ cup confectioners' sugar
1 tablespoon lemon juice

FILLING
2 pounds pears
¼ cup sugar
4 tablespoons flour
½ teaspoon grated lemon zest
3 tablespoons raisins or golden raisins
3 tablespoons chopped walnuts
½ teaspoon ground cinnamon

SERVES 6—8

1 Sift the flour and salt together into a mixing bowl. Rub in the butter, and stir in the walnuts and enough iced water to moisten. Gather into a ball, wrap, and refrigerate for 30 minutes. Preheat the oven to 375°F.

2 Make the filling. Peel the pears, and slice into a bowl. Add the sugar, flour and zest. Toss to coat the fruit. Add the raisins or golden raisins, walnuts and cinnamon. Mix lightly.

3 Roll out half the pastry on a lightly floured surface, and line a 9-inch pie plate that is 2 inches deep. Roll out the remaining pastry to an 11-inch round, and cut it into ½-inch wide strips. Spoon the filling into the pastry shell. Arrange the pastry strips on top, carefully weaving them in and out to make a lattice. Bake for 55 minutes or until golden.

4 Combine the confectioners' sugar, lemon juice and 1—2 teaspoons water in a bowl. Mix until smooth. Remove the pie from the oven, and drizzle the confectioners' sugar glaze over the top. Then let cool to lukewarm before serving.

93

Pumpkin Pie

INGREDIENTS

1 ¾ cups all-purpose flour
½ teaspoon salt
½ cup butter
2–3 tablespoons ice water
FILLING
¼ cup pecans, chopped
2 cups puréed pumpkin
2 cups light cream
¾ cup light brown sugar
¼ teaspoon salt
1 teaspoon ground cinnamon
½ teaspoon ground ginger
½ teaspoon ground cloves
¾ teaspoon grated nutmeg
2 eggs

SERVES 8

94

1 Preheat the oven to 425°F and sift together the flour and salt into a bowl. Rub in the butter, then add just enough ice water to make a firm dough.

2 On a lightly floured surface, roll out the dough to ¼ inch thick. Use it to line a 9-inch pie pan. Trim the excess dough.

3 Use the dough trimmings to make a decorative rope edge: Cut the dough into strips and twist together in pairs. Moisten the rim of the pie shell and press on the rope edge. Sprinkle the chopped pecans over the bottom of the pie shell.

4 With an electric mixer, beat together the puréed pumpkin, cream, brown sugar, salt, spices and eggs and pour the pumpkin mixture into the pie shell. Bake for 10 minutes, then reduce the heat to 350°F and continue baking for about 45 minutes until the filling is set. Let the pie cool in the pan, set on a wire rack.

Open Apple Pie

INGREDIENTS

2½ cups flour
½ teaspoon salt
½ cup refrigerated sweet butter, diced
¼ cup refrigerated shortening, diced
5–6 tablespoons iced water
FILLING
3 pounds sweet-tart firm eating or
cooking apples
¼ cup sugar
2 teaspoons ground cinnamon
grated zest and juice of 1 lemon
2 tablespoons butter, diced
2–3 tablespoons clear honey

SERVES 8

1 Sift the flour and salt together into a mixing bowl. Rub in the butter and shortening until the mixture resembles coarse bread crumbs. Stir in just enough iced water to moisten the dry ingredients, then gather together to make a ball. Wrap the pastry, and refrigerate for 30 minutes.

2 Preheat the oven to 400°F. Very lightly grease a deep 9-inch pie pan, and set aside. Peel, quarter and core the apples, then slice them into a bowl. Add the sugar, cinnamon, lemon zest and juice, and toss them together well.

3 Roll out the pastry on a lightly floured surface to a 12-inch round. Place the pastry over the pie pan so that the excess dough overhangs the edges. Fill with the apple mixture. Then fold in the pastry edges, crimping them loosely to make a decorative border. Dot the apples with the diced butter.

4 Bake the pie for about 45 minutes, until the pastry is golden, and the apples are tender. Melt the honey in a saucepan. Remove the pie from the oven, and immediately brush the honey over the apples to glaze. Serve warm or at room temperature.

95

Chocolate Cheesecake Pie

INGREDIENTS

1½ cups cream cheese, softened
4 tablespoons heavy cream
1 cup sugar
½ cup cocoa powder
½ teaspoon ground cinnamon
3 eggs
BASE
1½ cups graham cracker crumbs
8 amaretti cookies, crushed
(or extra graham cracker crumbs)
⅓ cup sweet butter, melted
DECORATION
whipped cream
chocolate curls

96

SERVES 8

1 Preheat the oven to 350°F. Make the base by mixing the crushed cookies with the melted butter. Press the mixture evenly over the bottom and sides of a 9-inch pie pan. Bake for 8 minutes, then let cool. Leave the oven on, and put a cookie sheet inside so that it heats up.

2 Beat the cheese and cream in a bowl with an electric mixer until smooth. Beat in the sugar, cocoa and cinnamon until blended. Then add the eggs, one at a time, beating for just long enough to combine. Pour the filling into the crumb shell, and bake on the hot cookie sheet for 25–30 minutes. The filling will sink as the cheesecake cools. Decorate with whipped cream and chocolate curls when cold.

Maple Pecan Pie

INGREDIENTS

1⅓ cups all-purpose flour
½ teaspoon salt
1 teaspoon ground cinnamon
½ cup butter
2–3 tablespoons ice water
FILLING
1 cup pecan halves
3 eggs, beaten
½ cup dark brown sugar
⅔ cup corn syrup
6 tablespoons maple syrup
½ teaspoon vanilla extract
¾ teaspoon salt

SERVES 8

97

1 Preheat the oven to 425°F. Make the pastry. Sift the flour, salt and cinnamon into a mixing bowl. Rub in the butter until the mixture resembles coarse crumbs. Sprinkle in the ice water, 1 tablespoon at a time, tossing lightly with your fingertips or a fork, until the dough clumps together and will form a ball.

2 On a lightly floured surface, roll out the dough to a circle 15 inches in diameter. Use it to line a 9-inch pie pan, easing in the dough and being careful not to stretch it. Make a fluted edge.

3 Using a fork, prick the bottom and sides of the pie shell all over. Bake for 10–15 minutes, until lightly browned. Cool, then sprinkle the pecans over the bottom of the shell. Reduce the oven temperature to 350°F.

4 Beat the eggs, sugar, syrups, vanilla extract and salt in a bowl. Pour over the pecans. Bake for about 40 minutes. Cool in the pan, on a wire rack.

Cherry Lattice Pie

INGREDIENTS

2 cups all-purpose flour
1 teaspoon salt
¾ cup butter or margarine, diced
4–5 tablespoons ice water
FILLING
1-pound can cherries, drained, or
4 cups pitted fresh cherries
6 tablespoons sugar
¼ cup flour
1½ tablespoons fresh lemon juice
¼ teaspoon almond extract
2 tablespoons butter or margarine

SERVES 8

1 Make the pastry. Sift the flour and salt into a mixing bowl. Rub in the butter or margarine until the mixture resembles coarse bread crumbs. Sprinkle in the ice water, 1 tablespoon at a time, tossing with your fingertips until the dough forms a ball.

2 Divide the dough in half and shape each half into a ball. On a lightly floured surface, roll out one of the balls to a circle about 12 inches in diameter.

3 Use the dough circle to line a 9-inch pie pan, easing the dough in and being careful not to stretch it. Trim all the excess dough, leaving a ½-inch overhang around the rim. Roll out the remaining dough to ⅛-inch thickness. With a sharp knife, cut out 11 strips, ½ inch wide.

4 In a mixing bowl, combine the cherries, sugar, flour, lemon juice and almond extract. Spoon the mixture into the pastry shell and dot the butter or margarine over the surface.

5 For the lattice, space five of the pastry strips over the cherry filling and fold every other strip back. Lay a strip across, perpendicular to the others. Fold  the strips back over the filling. Continue in this way, folding back every other strip each time you add a cross strip. Trim the ends of the lattice strips to make them even with the pastry overhang. Press together so that the edge rests on the rim of the pan. Flute the edge. Chill for 15 minutes. Preheat the oven to 425°F.

6 Bake the pie for 30 minutes, covering the edge with foil, if necessary, to prevent burning.

98

Peach Leaf Pie

INGREDIENTS

2 cups all-purpose flour
¾ teaspoon salt
⅔ cup cold butter, cut in pieces
5–6 tablespoons ice water
FILLING
2½ pounds ripe peaches, peeled and sliced
juice of 1 lemon
½ cup sugar
3 tablespoons cornstarch
¼ teaspoon grated nutmeg
½ teaspoon ground cinnamon
1 egg beaten with 1 tablespoon water, to glaze
2 tablespoons butter, diced
cream or ice cream, to serve

SERVES 8

1 Sift the flour and salt into a bowl. Rub in the butter, then stir in just enough ice water to bind the dough. Divide into two balls, one slightly larger than the other. Wrap and chill for at least 20 minutes. Preheat the oven to 425°F.

2 Combine the peaches with the lemon juice, sugar, cornstarch and spices. Set aside.

3 Roll out the larger dough ball thinly and line a 9-inch pie pan. Roll out the remaining dough. Cut out 3-inch leaves. Mark with veins.

4 Brush the bottom of the pie shell with egg glaze. Add the peaches, piling them high in the center. Dot with the butter. Starting from the rim, cover the peaches with concentric rings of leaves. Place tiny balls of dough in the center, if you like. Brush with the glaze. Bake for 10 minutes. Lower the heat to 350°F and bake for 35–40 more minutes. Serve hot or cold, with cream or ice cream.

100

Lemon Meringue Pie

INGREDIENTS

1¼ cups sugar
2 tablespoons cornstarch
pinch of salt
2 teaspoons finely grated lemon zest
½ cup fresh lemon juice
1 cup water
3 eggs, separated
3 tablespoons butter
9-inch pie shell, made from rich
shortcrust and baked blind

SERVES 6

1 Combine 1 cup sugar, the cornstarch, salt and lemon zest in a saucepan. Stir in the lemon juice and water until blended smoothly. Bring to a boil over medium-high heat, stirring constantly. Simmer for 1 minute, or until thickened.

2 Blend in the egg yolks. Cook over low heat for about 2 more minutes, stirring constantly. Remove from the heat. Add the butter and mix well.

3 Pour the lemon filling into the baked pie shell. Spread the filling evenly and level the surface. Cover tightly and let the pie cool completely. Preheat the oven to 350°F.

4 Beat the egg whites to soft peaks. Add the rest of the sugar and continue beating until the meringue is stiff and glossy.

5 Swirl the stiff meringue over the filling, sealing it to the rim of the pie shell. Bake for 10–15 minutes, or until the meringue is golden. Serve the pie cold.

Pear & Blueberry Pie

INGREDIENTS

2 cups all-purpose flour
pinch of salt
4 tablespoons vegetable shortening, cubed
4 tablespoons butter, cubed
FILLING
6 cups blueberries
2 tablespoons sugar
1 tablespoon arrowroot
2 ripe but firm pears, peeled, cored and sliced
½ teaspoon ground cinnamon
grated zest of ½ lemon
beaten egg, to glaze
sugar, for sprinkling
sour cream, to serve

SERVES 4

1 Sift the flour and salt into a bowl and rub in the shortening. Stir in 3 tablespoons cold water and mix to a dough. Chill for 30 minutes.

2 Place 2 cups of the blueberries in a pan with the sugar. Cover and cook gently until the blueberries have softened. Press through a sieve.

3 Blend the arrowroot with 2 tablespoons cold water and add to the blueberry purée. Place in a small saucepan and bring to a boil, stirring until thickened. Cool the mixture slightly.

4 Place a cookie sheet in the oven and preheat to 375°F. Roll out just over half the pastry on a lightly floured surface and use to line an 8-inch shallow pie pan or a heat proof plate; do this by flopping the pastry over the rolling pin and lifting it into position. Let the edges overhang.

5 Combine the remaining blueberries, the pears, cinnamon and lemon zest and spoon into the tin. Pour the blueberry purée over the top.

6 Roll out the remaining pastry to just larger than the pie pan and lay it over the filling. Press the edges together to seal, then trim off any excess pastry and crimp the edge. Make a small slit in the center to allow steam to escape. Brush with egg and sprinkle with sugar. Bake the pie on the hot cookie sheet for 40–45 minutes, or until golden. Serve warm with sour cream.

Mince Pies with Orange & Cinnamon Pastry

INGREDIENTS

1 ¼ cups mincemeat
beaten egg, to glaze
confectioners' sugar, for dusting
PASTRY
2 cups all-purpose flour
¼ cup confectioners' sugar
2 teaspoons ground cinnamon
¾ cup butter
grated zest of 1 orange
4 tablespoons iced water

MAKES 18

1 Sift together the flour, confectioners' sugar and cinnamon, then rub in the butter until the mixture resembles bread crumbs. Stir in the grated zest. Mix to form a dough with the iced water. Knead lightly, then roll out to a ¼-inch thickness. Using a 2½-inch round fluted cutter, stamp out 18 circles, re-rolling the dough as necessary.

2 Using a 2-inch round fluted cutter, stamp out 18 smaller circles.

3 Line two muffin pans with the 18 larger circles. Place a small spoonful of mincemeat into each pastry case and top with the smaller pastry circles, pressing the edges slightly together to seal in the filling. Cut a small steam vent in the top of each pie with a sharp knife.

4 Glaze the tops of the pies with egg and leave to rest in the refrigerator for 30 minutes. Preheat the oven to 400°F.

5 Bake the pies for 15–20 minutes until they are golden brown. Remove them to wire racks to cool. Dust with confectioners' sugar before serving.

Blueberry Pie

INGREDIENTS

*2 cups flour quantity shortcrust pastry
(see Pear & Blueberry Pie)
5 cups blueberries
¾ cup superfine sugar, plus extra
for sprinkling
3 tablespoons all-purpose flour
1 teaspoon grated orange zest
¼ teaspoon grated nutmeg
2 tablespoons orange juice
1 teaspoon lemon juice*

SERVES 6–8

1 Preheat the oven to 375°F. Roll out half the pastry and use to line a 9-inch pie pan that is about 2 inches deep.

2 Combine the blueberries, sugar, all-purpose flour, grated orange zest and nutmeg into a bowl. Toss the mixture gently to coat all the blueberries evenly. Tip the blueberry mixture into the pastry case and spread it evenly. Sprinkle over the citrus juices.

3 Roll out the remaining pastry and cover the pie. Cut out heart shapes, or cut two slits for releasing steam. Cut out small hearts from the trimmings to decorate the pie and finish the edge with a twisted pastry strip. Brush the top lightly with water and then sprinkle evenly with about 2 tablespoons of superfine sugar.

4 Bake the pie for about 45 minutes, or until the pastry is golden brown. Serve warm or cold.

Tarts & Cakes

From the elegant Raspberry & Hazelnut Meringue Cake to the extravagant White Chocolate & Strawberry Layer Cake, these will serve as the focal point of countless glamorous events.

Chocolate Apricot Linzer Tart

INGREDIENTS

2 cups dried apricots
½ cup orange juice
¾ cup water
3 tablespoons granulated sugar
3 tablespoons apricot jam
½ teaspoon ground cinnamon
½ teaspoon almond extract
½ cup chocolate chips
confectioners' sugar, for dusting
PASTRY
½ cup whole blanched almonds
½ cup granulated sugar
scant 2 cups all-purpose flour
2 tablespoons cocoa powder
1 teaspoon ground cinnamon
½ teaspoon salt
1 teaspoon grated orange zest
1 cup butter, diced
2–3 tablespoons ice water

SERVES 10–12

1 Mix the apricots, orange juice and water in a large pan. Bring them to a boil and simmer for 15–20 minutes, until the liquid is absorbed, stirring frequently to prevent sticking. Stir in the sugar, jam, cinnamon and almond extract, then purée in a food processor or press through a strainer.

2 Make the pastry. Process the almonds with half the sugar in the food processor, until finely ground. Sift the flour, cocoa, cinnamon and salt. Add to the processor with the remaining sugar and process to mix, then add the zest and butter and process for about 15 seconds, until the mixture resembles coarse crumbs. Pulse, adding just enough ice water to make the chocolate dough stick together.

3 Knead the dough lightly. With floured fingers, press half the dough onto the bottom and sides of a 10-inch springform pan. Prick the bottom with a fork, then chill the pie shell. Roll out the remaining dough between two sheets of plastic wrap to a 10-inch round; chill for about 30 minutes. Preheat the oven to 350°F.

4 Spread the filling in the pie shell and sprinkle with chocolate chips. Cut the dough into strips and arrange a lattice over the filling. Bake for 35–40 minutes, or  until the top of the pastry is set and the filling is bubbling. Cool slightly and remove the sides of the tin. Lay strips of paper across the lattice and dust with confectioners' sugar. Remove the paper carefully and slide the pie onto a serving plate.

Hazelnut Meringue Torte with Pears

INGREDIENTS

¾ cup granulated sugar
1 vanilla pod, split
2 cups water
4 ripe pears, peeled, halved and cored
6 egg whites
2½ cups confectioners' sugar
1¼ cups ground hazelnuts
1 teaspoon vanilla extract
2 ounces good-quality semisweet chocolate,
melted
chocolate shavings, to decorate
CHOCOLATE CREAM
2 cups whipping cream
10 ounces good-quality semisweet
chocolate, melted
4 tablespoons hazelnut-flavor liqueur

SERVES 8–10

1 In a pan large enough to hold the pears in a single layer, combine the sugar, vanilla pod and water. Bring to a boil, stirring until the sugar dissolves. Reduce the heat and add the pears. Cover and simmer for 12–15 minutes until tender. Remove from heat and let cool. Preheat the oven to 350°F.

2 Draw a 9-inch circle on two sheets of baking parchment and place on two cookie sheets.

3 Whisk the egg whites until soft peaks form, then gradually add the confectioners' sugar, whisking until stiff and glossy. Gently fold in the nuts and vanilla and spoon the meringue onto the marked circles. Bake for 1 hour. Turn off the heat and cool in the oven.

4 Slice the pear halves lengthwise. Then, make the chocolate cream. Beat the cream into soft peaks, then fold in the melted chocolate and liqueur. Put a third of the chocolate cream into an icing bag fitted with a star tip. Spread one meringue layer with half the remaining chocolate cream and top with half the pears. Pipe rosettes around the edge.

5 Top with the second meringue and the remaining chocolate cream and pear slices. Pipe rosettes around the edge. Drizzle the melted chocolate over the pears and decorate with the chocolate shavings. Chill for 1 hour before serving.

Raspberry & Hazelnut Meringue Cake

INGREDIENTS

4 egg whites
1 cup superfine sugar
few drops of vanilla extract
1 teaspoon malt vinegar
1 cup roasted chopped hazelnuts, ground
1¼ cups heavy cream
3 cups raspberries
confectioners' sugar, for dusting
mint sprigs, to decorate
SAUCE
2 cups raspberries
3–4 tablespoons confectioners' sugar
1 tablespoon orange liqueur

SERVES 6

1 Preheat the oven to 350°F. Baseline, and grease two 8-inch cake pans. Whisk the egg whites in a large bowl until stiff peaks form. Gradually whisk  in the superfine sugar. When stiff, gently fold in the vanilla, vinegar and nuts.

2 Divide the mixture between the pans, and bake for 50–60 minutes, or until they are crisp. Remove gently from the pans, and let cool on a wire rack.

3 Make the sauce. Purée the raspberries with the confectioners' sugar and liqueur in a food processor or blender. Press through a fine strainer into a pitcher. Refrigerate until ready to serve.

4 In a bowl, whip the cream to soft peaks. Gently fold in the raspberries. Place one round of meringue on a serving plate, and spread the raspberry and cream  mixture evenly over the top. Place the second round of meringue on top to form a sandwich.

5 Dust the top of the cake liberally with confectioners' sugar, and decorate with mint sprigs. Serve with the raspberry sauce. To cut the cake, use a large and very sharp knife.

Chocolate Pavlova with Chocolate Curls

INGREDIENTS

2½ cups confectioners' sugar
1 tablespoon unsweetened cocoa powder
1 teaspoon cornstarch
5 egg whites, at room temperature
pinch of salt
1 teaspoon cider vinegar or lemon juice
CHOCOLATE CREAM
6 ounces good-quality semisweet chocolate,
chopped
½ cup milk
2 tablespoons butter, cut into pieces
2 tablespoons brandy
2 cups heavy or whipping cream
TOPPING
4 cups mixed berries or diced mango, papaya,
lychees and pineapple
chocolate curls
confectioners' sugar

SERVES 8–10

1 Preheat the oven to 325°F. Place a sheet of baking parchment onto a cookie sheet and mark an 8-inch circle on it. Sift 3 tablespoons of the confectioners' sugar with the cocoa and cornstarch and set aside. Using an electric mixer, beat the egg whites until frothy. Add the salt and beat until the whites form stiff peaks.

2 Sprinkle the remaining confectioners' sugar into the egg whites, a little at a time, making sure each addition is blended in before beating in the next. Fold in the cornstarch mixture, then quickly fold in the vinegar or lemon juice.

3 Now spoon the mixture onto the paper circle, with the sides higher than the center. Bake for 1 hour, until set, then turn off the oven but leave the meringue  inside for 1 hour longer. Remove from the oven, peel off the paper and let cool.

4 Make the chocolate cream. Melt the chocolate in the milk over low heat, stirring until smooth. Remove from the heat and whisk in the butter and brandy. Cool for 1 hour.

5 Transfer the meringue to a serving plate. When the chocolate mixture has cooled, but is not too firm, beat the cream until soft peaks form. Stir half the cream into the chocolate mixture to lighten it, then fold in the remaining cream. Spoon it into the center of the meringue. Arrange fruit and chocolate curls in the center of the meringue, on top of the cream. Dust with confectioners' sugar and serve.

Chocolate Fudge Torte

INGREDIENTS

8 ounces bittersweet chocolate, chopped
1/2 cup sweet butter, diced
2/3 cup water
1 cup sugar
2 teaspoons vanilla extract
2 eggs, separated
2/3 cup sour cream
2 1/2 cups flour
2 teaspoons baking powder
1 teaspoon baking soda
pinch of cream of tartar
chocolate curls, raspberries and confectioners'
sugar, to decorate
CHOCOLATE FUDGE FILLING
1 pound bittersweet chocolate, chopped
1 cup sweet butter
5 tablespoons brandy
3/4 cup seedless raspberry preserve
GANACHE
1 cup heavy cream
8 ounces bittersweet chocolate, chopped
2 tablespoons brandy

SERVES 18–20

1 Preheat the oven to 350°F. Base-line, and grease a 10-inch springform pan. Place the chocolate, sweet butter and water in a pan. Heat gently, until melted.

2 Pour into a large bowl, and beat in the sugar and vanilla extract. Let cool, then beat in the egg yolks. Fold in the sour cream. Sift the dry ingredients, then fold them into the mixture. Whisk the egg whites in a bowl until stiff, and gently fold in.

3 Pour the mixture into the pan. Bake for 45–50 minutes. Let cool for 10 minutes, then remove from the pan. Let cool completely on a wire rack.

4 Make the fudge filling. Gently melt the chocolate and butter with 4 tablespoons of brandy. Set aside to cool. Meanwhile, cut the cake into three layers. Heat the preserve with the remaining brandy, and spread over each cake layer. Let set.

5 Return the bottom layer to the pan, and spread with half the filling. Top with the middle cake layer. Spread over the remaining filling, add the top cake layer, and press down gently. Refrigerate overnight.

6 Make the ganache. Bring the cream to a boil, remove from the heat, and stir in the chocolate, then the brandy. Strain, then set aside for 5 minutes to thicken. Remove the cake from its pan. Pour the ganache over the top, and cover the sides. Pipe any remaining ganache around the base of the cake using a star-shape nozzle. When set, decorate with chocolate curls, raspberries and confectioners' sugar. Do not refrigerate the glazed cake.

White Chocolate & Strawberry Torte

INGREDIENTS

4 ounces fine quality white chocolate, chopped
1/2 cup heavy cream
1/2 cup milk
1 tablespoon rum or vanilla extract
1/2 cup sweet butter, softened
3/4 cup superfine sugar
3 eggs
2 cups flour
1 teaspoon baking powder
pinch of salt
6 cups strawberries, sliced,
plus extra for decorating
3 cups whipping cream
2 tablespoons rum
WHITE CHOCOLATE MOUSSE FILLING
9 ounces fine quality white chocolate, chopped
1 1/2 cups whipping or heavy cream
2 tablespoons rum

SERVES 10

1 Preheat the oven to 350°F. Grease, and flour two 9-inch round cake pans, about 2 inches deep. Baseline the pans with nonstick parchment paper. Melt the chocolate in the cream in a double boiler over low heat, stirring until smooth. Stir in the milk and rum or vanilla extract. Set aside to cool.

2 Cream the butter and sugar until fluffy. Beat in the eggs one at a time. Sift together the flour, baking powder and salt. Stir into the egg mixture in batches, alternately with the melted chocolate, until just blended.

3 Divide the mixture between the pans. Bake for 20–25 minutes or until a cake tester inserted in the center of each cake layer comes out clean. Cool in the pans for 10 minutes. Turn out on to wire racks, peel off the parchment paper, and let cool.

4 Make the filling. Melt the chocolate with the cream in a saucepan over low heat, stirring frequently. Stir in the rum, and pour into a bowl. Refrigerate until just set, then whip the mixture lightly until it has a mousse-like consistency.

5 Slice each cake layer in half horizontally to make four layers. Spread a third of the mousse on top of one layer, and arrange a third of the strawberries over the mousse. Place another cake layer on top of the first, and cover with mousse and strawberries as before. Repeat this process once more, then top with the final cake layer.

6 Whip the cream with the rum. Spread about half the flavored cream over the top and sides of the cake. Use the remaining cream and strawberries to decorate the cake.

120

Orange & Apricot Roulade

INGREDIENTS

4 egg whites
½ cup raw superfine sugar
½ cup flour
finely grated zest of 1 small orange
3 tablespoons orange juice
confectioners' sugar, for dusting
shreds of orange zest, to decorate
FILLING
⅔ cup ready-to-eat dried apricots
⅔ cup orange juice

SERVES 6

1 Preheat the oven to 400°F. Grease a 13 x 9-inch jelly roll pan, and line it with a piece of nonstick parchment paper. Grease the paper well. Whisk the egg whites in a grease-free bowl until soft peaks form. Gradually add the superfine sugar, whisking hard after each addition, then gently fold in the flour, orange zest and juice.

2 Spoon the mixture into the prepared jelly roll pan, and spread it evenly. Bake for 15–18 minutes, or until the sponge is firm and pale golden in color.

Turn out on to a sheet of nonstick parchment paper. Working quickly, roll up the sponge loosely from one short side, and let cool.

3 Make the filling. Coarsely chop the apricots, and place them in a saucepan with the orange juice. Bring to simmering point, cover, and cook until most of the liquid has been absorbed. Purée the apricots in a food processor or blender. Cool.

4 Carefully unroll the roulade, and spread evenly with the apricot purée. Roll up again, and transfer to a platter. Arrange paper strips diagonally across the roll.

Sprinkle it lightly with confectioners' sugar, then carefully remove the paper to create the patterned effect. Decorate with orange zest, and serve.

122

Chocolate & Mint Fudge Cake

INGREDIENTS

6–10 mint leaves
¾ cup sugar
½ cup butter, plus extra for greasing
½ cup freshly made mashed potato
2 ounces semisweet chocolate, melted
1 ½ cups self-rising flour
pinch of salt
2 eggs, beaten
FILLING
4 mint leaves
½ cup butter
¾ cup confectioners' sugar
2 tablespoons chocolate mint liqueur
FUDGE TOPPING
1 cup butter
¼ cup sugar
2 tablespoons chocolate mint liqueur
2 tablespoons water
1 ¼ cups confectioners' sugar
¼ cup cocoa powder
pecan halves, to decorate

SERVES 8–10

124

1 Tear the mint leaves into pieces, and mix in a bowl with the sugar. Leave overnight.

2 Preheat the oven to 400°F. Grease and line an 8-inch cake pan. Sift the mint-flavored sugar and discard the mint leaves. Cream the butter and mint-flavored sugar with the mashed potato, then add the melted chocolate. Sift in half the flour with the salt, and add half the beaten eggs. Mix well. Add the remaining flour and eggs to the mixture.

3 Spoon the mixture into the prepared cake pan. Bake for 25–30 minutes, or until a cake tester inserted in the cake comes out clean. Turn the cake out on a wire rack. When cool, split into two layers.

4 Make the filling. Chop the mint leaves finely. Cream the butter, then mix in the confectioners' sugar and mint leaves to give a smooth buttercream. Sprinkle the liqueur over both layers of the cake, then sandwich them together with the filling.

5 Make the topping. Mix the butter, sugar, liqueur and water in a small saucepan. Heat until the butter and sugar have melted, then boil the mixture for 5 minutes. Sift the confectioners' sugar and cocoa into a large mixing bowl, and add the hot butter and liqueur mixture. Beat with a large spoon until cool and thick. Cover the cake with the fudge topping, and decorate with the pecan halves.

French Chocolate Cake

INGREDIENTS

1 cup unsalted butter, cut into pieces
9 ounces good-quality semisweet chocolate,
chopped
½ cup granulated sugar
2 tablespoons brandy or orange-flavor liqueur
5 eggs
1 tablespoon unbleached all-purpose flour
confectioners' sugar, to decorate
sour cream and fresh cherries, to serve

SERVES 10

126

1 Preheat the oven to 350°F. Line the bottom of a 9-inch springform pan with baking parchment. Wrap foil around the pan so it is water-tight.

2 Stir the butter, chocolate and granulated sugar over low heat until smooth. Cool slightly. Stir in the liqueur. In a bowl, beat the eggs lightly, then beat in the flour. Slowly beat in the chocolate mixture to blend. Pour into the pan. Smooth the surface.

3 Place the springform pan in a roasting pan. Fill the roasting pan with enough boiling water to come ¾ inch up the side of the springform pan. Bake for 25–30 minutes, until the edge of the cake is set, but the center is still soft. Remove the foil. Cool in the pan on a wire rack (the cake will sink and may crack).

4 Turn the cake upside-down onto a wire rack. Release the springform pan and remove the paper. The bottom of the cake is now the top.

5 Cut 6–8 strips of baking parchment 1 inch wide and place them randomly over the cake, or make a lattice-style pattern if you wish. Dust the cake with confectioners' sugar, then carefully remove the paper. Slide the cake onto a serving plate and serve with sour cream and fresh cherries.

Index